Unholy Charade

UNMASKING THE DOMESTIC ABUSER
IN THE CHURCH

Jeff Crippen

with Rebecca Davis

Justice Keepers Publishing
Tillamook, Oregon

Jeff Crippen with Rebecca Davis
Justice Keepers Publishing
www.cryingoutforjustice.com

Cover design: Kenny Crippen

Cover photography: Stephanie Council

All italicized first-person accounts not otherwise footnoted are published with written permission.

All Scripture quotations, unless otherwise noted, are from The Holy Bible, English Standard Version® (ESV®), copyright © 2001 by Crossway, a publishing ministry of Good News Publishers. Used by permission. All rights reserved.

Book Layout ©2013 BookDesignTemplates.com

Unholy Charade: Unmasking the Domestic Abuser in the Church/ Jeff Crippen with Rebecca Davis. —first edition

ISBN-13: 978-0692533222 (Justice Keepers Publishing)

ISBN-10: 0692533222

Second printing

Dedication

In the three years since *A Cry for Justice: How the Evil of Domestic Abuse Hides in Your Church!* was published, I have had the privilege of working with and learning from some of the finest Christian people I have ever known. With some of them I communicate nearly every week, sometimes every day. Even though I have never had the privilege of meeting most of them in person, I feel a deep connection with them.

At our blog, A Cry for Justice, www.cryingoutforjustice.com (ACFJ), we work to expose abusers who would parade themselves as Christians, interact with victims of abuse, and help them interact with one another in a safe environment. Many of these victims have suffered for twenty, thirty, forty, or more years through some of the most horrid evils you can imagine. In these pages you will read snapshots of some of their stories. They are the real heroes of our ministry at ACFJ.

It is to these people, who by the enabling grace and strength of Christ have persevered and conquered, that this book and our work are dedicated.

And they have conquered him by the blood of the Lamb and by the word of their testimony, for they loved not their lives even unto death. ~Revelation 12:11

Contents

Some important Scriptures
Why did God say "I hate divorce"? / I Corinthians 7

The "high view" of marriage
Who has the highest view? / Where the no-divorce for abuse position will lead / What about frivolous divorce? / Isn't it better for children to have both parents in the home?

Leave your church

Is the abuser a Christian?

Shining the light of truth on abuse and abusers
Hold to a Christ-like view of sin / Acknowledge the sin in the church / Prepare for reports of abuse / Preach against abuse / Changes in your church

Confronting the abuser
Handling a report of abuse / Questioning his relationship with Christ and others / Remember an abuser's ability to lie / Remember the pity play / Follow Nathan's example / Executing church discipline

A high calling
Stopping for the one / Validating her efforts to resist abuse / Changing her belief system / What will a pure, respectful wife do? / Be willing to go outside the camp / Be willing to be there for the long haul

Showing mercy
Listen to her / Understand abuse well enough to be able to believe her / Expose abuse for what it is / Take her side / Emphasize the justice of God / Don't take over her life / Expect trouble

Meeting her needs
Safety / Finances / Medical and legal needs / Mental health needs / Help with troubled children / Help in relating anew to God and others

Helping after the escape
Abuse through stalking / Abuse in spite of the restraining order / Abuse through custody battles / Abuse through visitation

Don't give up

The written Word is not sufficient for all understanding
The Bible is sufficient "for faith and life" / God also instructs through observation and experience / The place of psychology in life instruction

Jesus Christ, our true Deliverer
We cannot effect a complete rescue / The only One who can fully rescue / What does Christ's rescue look like? / The Just Judge will set things right

Acknowledgements

This book is the product of more than just my own hand. In particular I want to thank and recognize the faithful people of Christ Reformation Church whom I have had the privilege of serving as their pastor for over two decades. They have stood together for Christ's truth through many difficult trials and have embraced this ministry to abuse victims as their own mission. It is their support, prayers, and encouragement that have enabled me to write, blog, and speak to the issue of abusers hiding in the church and the injustice being dealt to abuse victims.

Also, my gratitude goes out to Rebecca Davis who has been a "right hand" in bringing this book into existence and who has a heart burning for justice for abuse victims.

Finally, I give many thanks to my fellow blog team members at A Cry for Justice: to Barbara Roberts and all the others who continue to provide me with encouragement as we strive to expose the evil of abuse for all to see.

The Lord Jesus Christ has done it all. Neither this book, my previous book, nor the ACFJ blog was planned by anyone. He has done it. To Him be all glory and praise and honor for raising us up to cry for justice for the widows and orphans of our day.

Foreword

by Katie Zerndt
domestic abuse survivor

Three years ago I found myself consumed with the realization that not only were my kids and I in real danger, but we were alone. Completely alone.

Ten years before, my husband had been arrested for domestic abuse. We had just moved to a new state where I knew no one. Over the years I reached out several times to my church for help, but each time I was told I needed to submit more and improve my relationship with God.

The years passed, and the religious guilt increased. I began to doubt that God even loved me. More babies came as the abuse amplified. Every time I reached out for help from my church, I was led to believe I was the problem. People even began to feel bad for my abuser, though I was the one coming to church hardly able to walk and weighing 72 pounds.

I fell into darkness as I gave in to the restraints my church and abuser had laid upon me. A vicious cycle of abuse, guilt, shame, and submission controlled me, until God brought some old friends back into my life, to stay with us for a week. It was so nice to have friends around, mainly because my husband was on his best behavior. That didn't fool my friends, though. God used them to confirm that I was being abused.

One day I took my five young children to the church playground. We were alone there, and I took the sweet moments of solitude while the kids played to search the internet for help. I knew the pain that my children and I were feeling was not right, but all I could hear was my pastor's voice ringing out that God hates divorce.

I came across a sermon series on Sermon Audio about domestic abuse. It was as if God led me right to it. I looked at the title of the first sermon: "Sin of Abuse Exposed by the Light of Christ." Sin? Surely I must not be in an abusive marriage? After all, my pastor knew what was going on—he wouldn't allow sin in my marriage! Would he?

The pastor on the audio sermon opened with a prayer, asking God to allow us to see sin for what it is, to withstand false teaching. I felt immediately God telling me that what I was experiencing was indeed abuse. It was indeed sin. And I was indeed a victim of false teaching.

I eagerly listened to all the audio sermons whenever it was safe to do so. Over the next few months God used the comforting voice of this amazing pastor to lead me through God's Word. I began to find hope in the Scriptures, something I had not felt in well over a decade.

Through the Scriptures and first-person accounts the audio pastor told, I realized not only was my husband abusive, but my church was not going to help. While this realization was painful, I was comforted as God continued to open my eyes. I soon began to see that even though the church had turned their back on me, God never has and never will!

I spent the next few years still struggling with fear and guilt. I was so afraid of being outside of God's will or angering God. I frequently went back to these sermons and the Scriptures.

I finally found the strength not only to leave my abuser, but also to begin to shed the years of religious guilt that had been heaved on me. Once I was able to focus on Christ rather than my abuser and my church, I was finally able to begin to experience Matthew 11:30— "For my yoke is easy and my burden is light."

Today my kids and I are free from our abuser, and we have moved on to a wonderful church. While the path has not been easy, He has never ceased to be a lamp unto my feet and a light unto my path.

It is awesome to look back and see God's hand at work, even in how I came to know the "audio pastor" that God used to lead me to see the truth of my abusive confinement.

I was introduced through the friend of a friend to a dear woman named Rebecca who was working on a book about domestic abuse. While we were together I told her of an amazing sermon series that had helped me to overcome the restrictions of false religious guilt to finally free my children and me from the bondage of abuse. As I pulled up the series, she laughed. I quickly joined her as she clued me into the fact that Jeff Crippen—the pastor I had listened to for so long—was the same man who was the author of the book she was working on! This is truly the work of an omnipotent, loving God. He knows your pain. He knows your battles. You are not alone. He is with you.

I was blessed to have been able to read this manuscript. Pastor Crippen's personal crusade to end this hidden sin within the church is like none other. God is using him in a mighty way.

The power of abusers hiding in our churches is real, and their dominance only continues to grow as we continue to turn a blind eye to their sin. Don't be fooled; this evil can be hiding in your church! They can be sitting in the pew next to you. They are wicked men. The church has become their playground and the Bible their weapon of choice. It is so important to recognize these wolves in sheep's clothing before they completely destroy the foundation of love in the church. The effects of their abuse will poison generations to come.

I myself am one of the once-broken voices you will hear from in this book's first-person accounts. I knew the struggles of David as he fled for his life from Saul. My cries echoed his as my abuser accosted me in the shadows.

The Spirit-led words of this book have brought me peace and understanding. My prayer is that every church leader, elder, and abuse victim would read Pastor Crippen's erudite words. Please take time to read how these depraved minds work to destroy the beauty God has created. Learn how to help. Unmask this Unholy Charade.

His steadfast servant,

Katie Zerndt

Psalm 91:14-15

"Because he loves me," says the Lord, "I will rescue him;
I will protect him, for he acknowledges my name.
He will call on me, and I will answer him;
I will be with him in trouble, I will deliver him and honor him.
With long life I will satisfy him
and show him my salvation."

Introduction

My own journey

In my first book, *A Cry for Justice: How the Evil of Domestic Abuse Hides in Your Church!* I described my own journey of understanding about abuse. I explained that I began with research about sexual abuse because of a case in our church, and then broadened my understanding to examine domestic abuse. As I researched patterns of abusive behavior, I began to realize that as a pastor I had been the target of abusers in local churches I had served through the years.

In the early years of my pastoral ministry, abusive men and women dominated, seeing themselves as entitled to power and control. Though I didn't understand it, the abuse affected me so deeply that after several years of it, when someone outside my family was kind to me, it seemed like a foreign thing. Eventually I realized that I had been isolated and robbed of any confidence that other people would ever want to have a relationship with me. When I finally told someone my story, he affirmed me and then said, "You and your wife are incredibly wounded people." I didn't understand what he meant at the time, but years later as I researched the topic, those words came back to me and made sense.

As I learned about the tactics of abusers and their effect on the church, I began to share my insights. Eventually I preached a sermon series about domestic abuse at my church, which I called "The Psychology of Sin." Reactions were mixed, to put it mildly. They ranged from extreme gratefulness and excitement to anger that I would actually preach such a series.

This sermon series was posted online at Sermon Audio,[1] where more people heard it than I would have imagined. That series became the foundation for my first book, *A Cry for Justice.* Three more years of hearing people's personal testimonies and coming to even greater understanding of the nature and dynamics of abuse and its effects on the victims have resulted in this second book.

On our blog, www.cryingoutforjustice.com, I have interacted with many abuse victims, their friends and relatives, a few abusers, and many others. Since most of the victims who contact us at ACFJ are Christians, the favorite chosen façade of their abusers is one of pious, saintly, eminent "Christianity." These abusers who day after day cruelly abuse their families and yet show up at their local church on Sunday playing their various chosen roles (poor victim, suffering saint, man of God, wonderful Christian who intensely loves the Lord) are, in my opinion, the most hard-hearted of any hard-hearted sinners I have ever seen. It would not surprise me at all when we stand before the Lord at the final judgment to learn that these wicked ones were indeed "Esaus," people for whom repentance was impossible, so knowingly did they trample underfoot the blood of Christ.[2]

As I have worked to expose abusers and cry out for justice for the victims, I have come under attack. But in over thirty years of pastoral work, I've never experienced anyone more grateful or enthusiastic than these unsung heroines (and sometimes heroes) who have endured so much. If our churches could be full of Christians who have endured this kind of suffering, as well as others who intensely loved Christ and embraced them in their suffering, there would be no stopping us. We would be a dynamic and fearless bunch, and a church body that would be heaven to lead.

In fact, I have found just such a church. When I came to Christ Reformation Church here in Oregon twenty-two years ago, I remember praying, "Lord, please make this church and this pastorate the 'golden' one of my service for you." Golden it is, and the Lord brought it about in

---

[1] www.sermonaudio.com/crc.
[2] Hebrews 6:4ff.

a way I never would have imagined—through ministry to the victims of this evil and through exposure of those who abuse them. This is a dynamic group, having persevered with Christ through many battles.

We also have an extended congregation worldwide, who listen to our sermons, read our books, visit our blog, and stand together with us in this great work of the Lord. We invite you to read, learn, and come join us in the fight as we expose the hypocrites, cry out for God's justice for the oppressed, and take the light of the Father of Lights into a dark world.

Using the term "victim"

The debate is ongoing over whether to use *victim* or *survivor* to refer to people who have come out of abusive relationships. Each author has to make a choice as to which term he will use.

Many of the people I write for are still in their abusive relationships. They are still, without a doubt, victims. Even those who have come out of situations of domestic abuse can take a very long time to understand that they have been victimized. I use the term not to demean anyone or to promote a victim mentality, but simply to help survivors of abuse come to understand that they have been victimized, and that this victimization has had profound effects upon them.

Regarding my choices of pronouns in this book, I do know that women can be sociopaths and narcissists and abusers too, and I do know some men who are genuine abuse victims of their wives. A few of the first-person accounts in this book are victims of abusive wives or mothers. But the fact is that abuse is primarily a male problem. For this reason, and because of the problem of women being forced to submit to abusers in our churches, and also just to keep things simpler, in this book I use the feminine pronoun for the victim and masculine for the abuser.

CHAPTER 1

A Charade is Playing Out in Our Midst

Beware of false prophets, who come to you in sheep's clothing but inwardly are ravenous wolves. You will recognize them by their fruits. Are grapes gathered from thornbushes, or figs from thistles? So, every healthy tree bears good fruit, but the diseased tree bears bad fruit.[3]

Abusers in the Scriptures

"His speech was smooth as butter, yet war was in his heart; his words were softer than oil, yet they were drawn swords."[4] The Psalmist knew all too well from hard experience how charming an abuser can be in order to ensnare a victim. As one author put it, "His inordinately attentive, charming, and tempting behavior cannot be considered anything more than bait."[5]

I Samuel 9:2 tells us that Saul was handsome with a kingly bearing. But in chapter 13 when Saul offered a sacrifice against the Lord's command, he showed himself to be manipulative and self-serving, minimizing his faults and blaming others. Chapter 18 shows when Saul

---

[3] Matthew 7:15-17.

[4] Psalm 55:21.

[5] Sarah Braun and Bridget Flynn, *Honeymoon and Hell: A Memoir of Abuse* (Sarah Braun, 2010), Location 771, Kindle edition.

perceived David as a threat to his own kingship, he targeted the younger man as his victim. Saul became paranoid, envious, and murderous.

Hebrews 6:4-8 first speaks of "those who have once been enlightened, who have tasted the heavenly gift, and have shared in the Holy Spirit and have tasted the goodness of the word of God and the powers of the age to come." It then says if they "have fallen away, [it is impossible] to restore them again to repentance." He then compares their hard hearts to hard ground that bears thorns and thistles. Who are these whose hearts are too hard to bear any kind of fruit?

The people who are secretly practicing evil
while playing the game of pretend as good Christians
are the hardest and most treacherous of all abusers.
When a person decides to use the mask of Christianity for his
unholy charade, he commits an odious sin.

The passage in Hebrews goes on to say they are "crucifying once again the Son of God to their own harm and holding him up to contempt." These abusers, by their evil façade, mock Christ. They might as well have been standing in the crowd of mockers at the crucifixion.

The wolf in the flock

In order to successfully satisfy his lust for power and control, an abuser may possess great wealth or political power. Throughout world history, abusers have risen to power and wreaked havoc on millions.

Though abusers in our churches have a smaller sphere of control, they have a similar lust for power. They will commonly find their power through an outstanding ability to play the hypocrite, especially in the church, often feigning impressive characteristics of Christianity very convincingly. At the same time, they will wreak havoc on spouses and children, as well as others under their authority.

The Apostle Paul warned the Ephesians that wolves in sheep's clothing would come into their midst. But what does one of these fierce wolves look like?

He looks just like everyone else, *because he's wearing sheep's clothing.* The abuser, who in reality is characterized by selfishness, manipulation, and irresponsibility, often presents to the church as a model Christian and a good husband. In fact, evil people really do have the ability to present themselves as the nicest, most charismatic, most caring people you'll ever want to meet.

Most of the abuse victims who contact us through our blog, A Cry for Justice, are Christians whose abusers have made a show of Christianity. Numbers of these wolves in wool are pastors, elders, missionaries, or "eminent saints" with reputations as stalwart church members, supposedly ready to give themselves to Christ's work more than anyone else in the church.

> *When I met my abusive husband, he was an usher and taught Sunday school. The church members spoke so highly of him. They said he was the "big toe" of the church—the church depended on him to keep going.*

These wolves find it relatively easy to dress like sheep, claiming to believe all the orthodox doctrine, which is easy to do. What he does in secret, though, is put false doctrine into practice.

Robert Louis Stevenson's classic novel *The Strange Case of Dr. Jekyll and Mr. Hyde* provides the terminology we often use to describe abusers. The same man who is a cruel abuser in private (Mr. Hyde) can appear in public as a respectable, normal, sociable Christian gentleman (Dr. Jekyll).

"His most consistent feature . . . is his apparent normality. Ordinary concepts of psychopathology fail to define or comprehend him. This idea is deeply disturbing to most people. How much more comforting it would be if the perpetrator were easily recognizable, obviously deviant or disturbed. But he is not." [6]

---

[6] Judith Herman, *Trauma and Recovery: The Aftermath of Violence—from Domestic Abuse to Political Terror* (Basic Books, 2015), pp 74-75.

Christians are gullible

Another factor working in the abuser's favor is the fact that many Christians, though in theory they believe in "the exceeding sinfulness of sin,"[7] in practice believe that everyone is basically good, or at least that we all struggle with sin in basically the same way and feel the same kind of guilt about it. Average people find it nearly impossible to bring themselves to believe that anyone could function without a conscience,[8] or if there is such a person, he couldn't be in *our* church. No one could really be practicing hypocrisy in our church to such a degree that he is actually a wolf looking like a sheep.

This is a very naïve way of thinking, because as the Bible teaches and as this book will show, this is simply not true.

In addition, in *The Sociopath Next Door*, author Martha Stout warns that physical appearance bears too much weight in the judgments most of us make about others.[9] The abuser counts on such things as his charming personality, handsome physical appearance, generous donations, unusual dedication in religious practices, above-average intelligence, and eloquent words to attract enablers to himself.

When a wolf tells you that he would never do such a thing as eat a sheep (and besides it was all the sheep's fault anyway), he can sound very plausible.[10] Because of that, we fall asleep guarding the ones we've been entrusted to care for. Speaking of the sociopath, who is far more common than many of us realize, Martha Stout says

"He lies artfully and constantly, with absolutely no sense of guilt that might give him away in body language or facial expression."[11]

---

[7] A quotation from Jeremiah Burroughs, Puritan author.
[8] Robert D. Hare, *Without Conscience: The Disturbing World of the Psychopaths Among Us* (The Guilford Press, 1999), Location 2406, Kindle edition.
[9] Martha Stout, *The Sociopath Next Door* (Three Rivers Press, 2005), p 93.
[10] Skilled abusers can even convince professional counselors that the counselors don't need to listen to the victim's side of the story.
[11] Stout, *The Sociopath Next Door,* p 43.

Confronted with such a character, the normal person might find the facts stated by the culprit to be conflicting or illogical, but will quickly cast any doubts aside because "surely no one could lie with such sincerity."

One important truth we will all do well to remember, though, is that good people do not pretend to be bad, but bad people very often pretend to be good. When a person displays different personalities, remember that the evil one is the real person.

No excuse for being naïve

A man may speak eloquently on the merits of Jesus Christ or the superiority of the New Covenant over the Old. He may be able to explain why one view of end times is to be believed. He may clearly articulate why his chosen mode of baptism is to be preferred. But Christians should know that a man's Christianity is not to be judged by his ability to lead an intellectual Bible study. Christ has told us all about such people who claim they love God. "You will recognize them by their fruits."[12] This includes not only the actions that everyone can see, but the life that is lived behind closed doors at home.

Christians have no excuse for being so naïve about evil. Even though you may think you could never play the hypocrite to that extent, you must also be willing to recognize the truth that God's Word shows us: human beings are capable of incredible degrees of evil and deception, and an abusive person can do such things with no remorse at all. The Word of God teaches that such deception is not only possible, but likely, no matter how disturbing it is to acknowledge.

To deny that this kind of evil can happen, does happen, and might even be happening in "good families" in your own congregation is to embrace a dangerous dream world from which you desperately need to awaken.

---

[12] Matthew 7:16a

We must put away our preconceived notions and superficial, rushed, and simplistic study of the Bible, humbly admitting that we have much to learn, and seeking God's help as we delve into Scriptures that we have never truly understood or fully believed. When we study this evil called abuse, we are studying one of the clearest illustrations of the very nature of sin. This is one of the primary reasons that I spent twenty-one Sundays with my congregation preaching and teaching on this topic. It is not a mere "social" issue, suitable only for those liberal social-gospel churches. It is the embodiment of much of what the Bible reveals to us about sin. One of the things God's Word warns us about in respect to sin is that it is deceptive in its very essence.

If you are ready to do battle with sin, meet the abuser. Learn about him—how he thinks, what his tactics are, and what he does to his victims. Then learn what to do about the evil and how you can best help the victims of his abuse. There are few better ways to learn to be like Jesus Christ.

CHAPTER 2

The Mind Behind the Charade

How do we understand abuse?

If someone asked you to define abuse, you might describe the visible acts of physical violence, things you can see from the outside, objectively. But these outward acts are only the evil fruits of a much deeper root, what I would call the essence of abuse.

Abuse, in its essential being, resides in the *mentality* and *mindset* of the abuser, in the paradigm through which he sees himself, his world, and most importantly, his victim. Until we enter the abusive mind, we will be unable to understand and expose abusers and unable to give victims the help they need.

The fundamental characteristic of an abuser: no conscience

> *Your tongue plots destruction,*
> *like a sharp razor, you worker of deceit.*
> *You love evil more than good,*
> *and lying more than speaking what is right. Selah.*
> *You love all words that devour,*
> *O deceitful tongue.*[13]

---

[13] Psalm 52:2-4.

The Bible teaches that all people are created in the image of God. As part of that image, our Creator has given each of us the knowledge of certain basic truths. We know that we are created beings[14] who are accountable to our Creator. We know that we owe Him not only our acknowledgment that He is God, but also our love and service. We also owe love to our fellow human beings.[15] As Christians, we have these two greatest commandments written upon our hearts: to love God and to love others. But as part of God's endowment to all people, He has given each of us an internal judge called a conscience. This conscience, though, does not exist in isolation,[16] as author Martha Stout so well puts it. "Conscience does not exist without an emotional bond to someone or something, and in this way conscience is closely allied with the spectrum of emotions we call 'love.'"[17]

> *Looking back, I will never forget a discussion we had had when we were still married. I spoke of the unbelievable love I felt for our children, my astonishment that these were my own. I had won a lottery of sorts and wouldn't hesitate to give my life to save theirs. He, in turn, spoke of not really knowing what love meant or felt like. The important thing, he said, was to act in a godly manner even if the feelings were not present. It felt, even then, that we were shouting across an abyss, unable to understand or reach each other.*

The primary factor distinguishing a hypocritical abuser from other people is that in an abuser, the conscience is either remarkably weak or possibly even non-existent.

This lack of conscience is the most important key to understanding the abusive mind.

Other fundamental attitudes spring out of this void of conscience, attitudes that a healthy conscience would condemn. Though his public

---

[14] Psalm 100:3.
[15] Matthew 22:37-40.
[16] Romans 1:16ff.
[17] Stout, *The Sociopath Next Door*, pp 25-26.

life may look self-sacrificing, the abuser lives with no love except for himself, thinking and acting without a normal concept of self-giving love. His attitude is that the universe and everyone in it exists for his pleasure, service, and glory.

When an abuser is unmasked, people can be inclined to feel sorry for him, believing that the weight of his misdeeds has pressed him down. "Yes, he did wrong, but surely he has suffered terrible internal torment all these years." But this kind of thinking assumes that the abuser is indeed "weighed down" by his conscience, as the average person would be if we did such things. However, because the abuser doesn't have a healthy, functioning conscience, the result is that he doesn't lose any sleep at all over his wrongdoings.

> *My abuser could curse, scream, and hit his son, and then go right to sleep, peacefully.*

When does a sinful human being become an abuser? Though the way the abuse is expressed can vary widely, its essence can be reduced to

(1) absence of an active conscience, which will naturally result in

(2) certain strongholds and characteristics, which will then lead to

(3) certain actions.[18]

Strongholds and characteristics

The Bible teaches that spiritual fortresses, or strongholds, are lofty opinions that are "raised against the knowledge of God."[19] Consider some of the strongholds in the abuser's mind:

He holds a sense of tremendous **entitlement**. He believes he deserves to be served, and his victims are here on this earth for his pleasure.

His mission in life is to **control** others, especially his spouse and children, for his own selfish ends. He sees his victims as ones who must be dominated and conquered. He takes pleasure in exerting **power** over them.

---

[18] The strongholds and characteristics are addressed in this chapter. The actions will be addressed in the following two chapters.

[19] II Corinthians 10:4-5.

He feels *justified* in doing whatever he "needs" to do in order to accomplish his desires. In true Machiavellian style, he views "truth" as relative and "reality" as his own perspective, both of which can be molded and modified for his own purposes.

In his excellent book *Character Disturbance*, George Simon observes:

> Many [abusive] behaviors traditionally thought of as unconscious mental processes designed to prevent pangs of conscience are better viewed as *conscious and deliberate acts.* They're done so frequently and without compunction that they become routine or "automatic." They obstruct the internalization of pro-social values (i.e., enable the person to avoid responsibility), as well as provide a means to effectively manipulate and control others.[20]

An abuser also lacks qualities we would expect to find in normal people:

He has no *empathy*. He cannot share in the feelings of others (though he can imitate these feelings when it suits his purposes).

He lacks *shame*. He has no sense of wrongdoing (though he can display false repentance convincingly when it suits his purposes).

He experiences little or no real *fear* or anxiety.

Our definition of abuse

With the foregoing facts in mind, here is the definition of abuse that we offer at our blog, A Cry for Justice:

> Abuse is a mentality of entitlement and superiority that evidences itself in the various tactics the abuser uses to obtain and enforce unjustified power and control over another person. The abuser thinks that he is absolutely justified in using these tactics to maintain this power and control. Abuse is effected in many ways: both physical (including sexual) and non-physical (verbal and emotional). It can be active (physically or verbally)

---

[20] George K. Simon, Ph.D., *Character Disturbance: the phenomenon of our age* (Parkhurst Brothers, 2011), Locations 1721-1727, Kindle edition. Italics added.

or passive (not speaking, not acting). Abuse, therefore, is not limited to physical assault.

All abusers share the characteristics mentioned in this chapter, but not all abusers operate at the same level of intensity. Largely according to the degree of dysfunction of their conscience, abusers will fall somewhere in a range or scale of abuse. For example, every abuser will be remarkably selfish. But further up the scale of intensity, we will see a narcissistic personality. The most severe types of abusers classify as sociopaths or psychopaths,[21] people who, among other traits, appear to have no spark of conscience at all.

Psychopaths have a narcissistic and grossly inflated view of their self-worth and importance, a truly astounding egocentricity and sense of entitlement, and see themselves as the center of the universe, as superior beings who are justified in living according to their own rules.[22]

As you read the following descriptions of abusers, keep in mind the matter of degrees. A person doesn't have to be only on the most extreme end of the spectrum in order to qualify as an abuser. For example, while some abusers physically beat their victim, others abuse passively by refusing to work.

As time passes, an individual abuser can advance along this scale and become a greater and greater danger to his victim.

The abusive mindset

Entitlement

The mindset that encompasses the essence of abuse is a citadel of egocentric, narcissistic entitlement. The abuser's world is about him and for him. He is the center of his own universe. He has no interest in the Scripture's instructions to love and care for others. Like Satan, he declares in just about every word and action, "I will be like the Most

---

[21] These terms are used more or less interchangeably.

[22] Hare, *Without Conscience*, p. 38.

High,"[23] and he loves the serpent's promise to Adam and Eve, "you shall be like God."[24] Though Bancroft and Silverman apply the following words to batterers, they would apply as well to all kinds of abusers:

> Entitlement is the belief that one has special rights and privileges without accompanying reciprocal responsibilities. . . . A primary manifestation of entitlement is that batterers expect family life to center on the meeting of their needs, often to the point of treating their partners like servants. . . . They may believe that they are owed services and deference without regard to their own level of contribution or sacrifice.[25]

Power and control

Because abusive people think in grandiose terms of entitlement and superiority about themselves, it's not surprising that an abusive person would disdain the opposite sex, and especially his or her victim.

A domestic abuser thinks of his victim as a possession like a car or a house, an object to be used for the pleasure of the owner, stripped of humanity and personhood. For example, if his wife is beautiful, an abuser might refer to her as a "trophy wife," something that has been won and is now possessed. As the abuser continues in his delusion of seeing his victim as an object instead of a valuable person made in the image of God, his abuse can also increase. Because the abuser sees his victim as an object to be used however he pleases, his attitudes and actions seem to him to be only reasonable, so he feels no qualms or scruples about his abuse.[26]

The abuser believes that he deserves to have others acknowledge his power and control over them. If his victim refuses to submit to his rule, then he believes that he bears no fault in using abusive tactics to make

---

[23] Isaiah 14:14.

[24] Genesis 3:5.

[25] Lundy Bancroft and Jay G. Silverman, *The Batterer as Parent: Addressing the Impact of Domestic Violence on Family Dynamics* (Sage Publications, 2002), pp 8-9.

[26] King Ahasuerus' treatment of Queen Vashti is a perfect example. This story is told in Esther chapter 1.

her bow to him. None of this unpleasantness would need to happen, he reasons, if she would just respect and obey him.

Justification

The abuser's mind exercises impressive illogic in justifying a flagrant double standard between himself and his victim. What he sees in her as a grossly stupid error or even downright mean crime, is for him simply a small slip-up.

In other words, the abuser sees the speck in his victim's eye while justifying the log in his own.

The abusive mind cannot conceive the notion of entertaining the remote possibility that he could ever be the problem. Even if witness after witness were to testify to his abusive ways, he would blame and accuse rather than admitting fault. He justifies, drawing upon his uncanny ability to make excuses.

> Disturbed characters always have an answer for everything. Challenge them and they'll come up with a litany of reasons why their behavior was justified. In my work with disordered characters, I've heard literally thousands of preposterous excuses for irresponsible behavior.[27]

Two-year-old tantrums

Despite the abuser's ability to masquerade as a fine Christian, these mindsets of entitlement and justification can cause his domestic behavior to be overtly childish. In his childishness the abuser is easily distracted from one unfinished project to another. If he is sick or experiences a minor injury or even an inconvenience, he'll demand that everyone in the family focus on him. In his childishness, he will make irrational statements, contradict himself, refuse to be corrected, and blame and accuse when confronted. When he doesn't get his way, he will throw a tantrum.

---

[27] Simon, *Character Disturbance*, Locations 1778-1780, Kindle edition.

> *The last time I rode in a vehicle with him, we planned to Christmas shop for the kids together, and he promised that he would not get upset. It went okay until I got a text and wouldn't share it with him. Yelling in the store, making the other customers stare, stomping off to sit in one of the displays and cry, all on a day he promised not to get upset. We were separated at the time, and it seemed like he just could not cope with not being the one in control of everything anymore. When things finally settled down and we started home from the city, he ranted the entire hour. I remember thinking that if I jumped from the car on the highway, I wouldn't have to live like this anymore.*

Of course, when a two-year-old throws a tantrum, he has no strength to throw anyone on the floor but himself. An adult abuser, on the other hand, can throw family members to the floor or against a wall. This is how the mind of the two-year-old terror becomes dangerous. Imagine a person with the emotional maturity of a two-year-old but with the resources of an adult—strength, money, devious cleverness, ability to manipulate. Imagine him with a gun.

Many victims have testified that their abuse intensified when they were pregnant. This is an example of the "toddler" being jealous of the new baby. During the pregnancy, his wife has new needs—vitamins, doctor appointments, more rest, perhaps a special diet. None of these needs fit into the abuser's world. Pregnant women have suffered horribly at the hands of abusive men.

No empathy

Empathy is the ability to understand and appreciate the feelings of others, the ability to see a situation through another's eyes. But frequently, abuse victims will describe "those eyes," referring to the blank, cold, soul-less stare of a person with no empathy. This lack of empathy is what causes abusers to be seemingly incapable of seeing themselves for what they really are.[28]

---

[28] Lundy Bancroft, *When Dad Hurts Mom: Helping Your Children Heal the Wounds of Witnessing Abuse* (Berkley Books, 2004), p 296.

> *I first became aware that some piece of him was missing was when, a year into marriage, I feared that I might have miscarried. I recall sobbing in the bathtub, aching for a baby. His words were far from consoling: "I'm relieved it turned out this way: we would have had to cancel the trip we were planning."*

In *Physical Abusers and Sexual Offenders: Forensic and Clinical Strategies,* Scott Allen Johnson delineates three aspects of empathy: cognitive recognition, emotional connection, and behavioral demonstration.

> *[C]ognitive recognition* involves understanding the concept of being a victim, that is, to appreciate what victims of abuse experience. . . . *Emotional connection* refers to experiencing and being able to identify the guilt, shame, and fear that the abuser's behavior has caused his victim. . . . *Behavioral demonstration . . .* means that you will do what you say you will do and behave in ways that live up to and demonstrate your beliefs, morals, and values.[29]

Without empathy, a person can never understand Jesus' command "do unto others as you would have them do unto you."[30] Abuse victims may think, "If only I could get him to see how he has hurt me," but this assumes that the abuser is willing to see a situation through another person's eyes. When he has just screamed foul language at his victim and she tries to get him to see her perspective, he might say, "You're blowing this thing all out of proportion. I was joking. Can't you take a joke?"

> *On the day we told our kids that we were getting a divorce, we had the strangest conversation. My husband knew that I was asking for a divorce because of abuse and control issues (we had received many hours of counselling that had made no difference at all), and when the kids left the room he said to me, "The thing is I knew that I was hurting you. It's just that I didn't care." He then said, "I know it's kind of weird, but could you comfort me?"*

[29] Scott Allen Johnson, *Physical Abusers and Sexual Offenders: Forensic and Clinical Strategies* (CRC Press, 2006), p. 65. Italics added.
[30] Matthew 7:12.

No shame, no regret

When you read the following chapters, you may recoil at some of the things abusers do to their victims. If so, you have an appropriate sense of what we call shame, "the right perception of what is improper or disgraceful."[31] You may think, "How can one person do those things to another person?" But this mindset assumes that the abuser's healthy conscience will feel "the painful emotion arising from the consciousness of something dishonoring, ridiculous, or indecorous in one's own conduct. . . ."[32] Just as Judas felt no shame when he kissed Jesus, an abuser can commit shocking abuse and then act as if nothing serious has happened.

At times, an abuser may actually *appear* to sense some regret regarding his abuse.[33] But it is an ephemeral regret that vaporizes without producing real change, as his true characteristics come forward once again. More likely his show of repentance and remorse is an act designed to manipulate his victim or those who have been told about his abuse.[34]

No fear

Because the abuser lacks an active conscience, because he carries a tremendous sense of entitlement, power, and justification, because he has no love for anyone except himself, no empathy, and no shame, his fear of consequences is greatly diminished or even non-existent. His exalted sense of self places himself above every kind of law, including safety rules, civil and criminal laws, and even God's moral codes. Respecting only his own rules, the abuser rejects any other law.

Some abusers join anti-government organizations, intent on defending the rights and liberties of the Constitution as true patriots. The abuser, though, grants no bill of rights to his victim but instead strips her of her freedom and humanity.

---

[31] *Oxford English Dictionary* (Oxford University Press, 2015), definition of *sense of shame*.
[32] Ibid., definition of *shame*.
[33] This is often part of the cycle of abuse, described later in this chapter.
[34] The concept of repentance is explored further in chapter 6.

Even though victims have reported that threatening their abuser with the police sometimes does seem to restrain him, there is still no *inner* acknowledgment that his actions have been wrong. Though the law may supply an external restraint through its penalties, he still sees it as an opponent to be conquered.

Perhaps it goes without saying that the primary fear missing in the life of the abuser is the fear of God. His thinking matches the thinking of the wicked described in Psalm 36:1-4.

> *Transgression speaks to the wicked deep in his heart;*
> *there is no fear of God before his eyes.*
> *For he flatters himself in his own eyes*
> *that his iniquity cannot be found out and hated.*
> *The words of his mouth are trouble and deceit;*
> *he has ceased to act wisely and do good.*
> *He plots trouble while on his bed;*
> *he sets himself in a way that is not good;*
> *he does not reject evil.*

The cycle of abuse

> *Make no friendship with a man given to anger,*
> *nor go with a wrathful man,*
> *lest you learn his ways and entangle yourself in a snare.*[35]

In his seminal work *Why Does He Do That? Inside the Minds of Angry and Controlling Men,* Lundy Bancroft describes what he and several other professionals in the field have recognized as the cycle of abuse.

> Life with an abuser can be a dizzying wave of exciting good times and painful periods of verbal, physical, or sexual assault. The longer the relationship lasts, the shorter and farther apart the positive periods tend to become. If you have been involved with an abusive partner for many years, the good periods may

---

[35] Proverbs 22:24-25.

have stopped happening altogether, so that he is an unvarying source of misery.[36]

The cycle of abuse has been observed by many abuse victims and analysts. Variations of it, some even more detailed, can be found in chart form at most domestic violence websites and are often called "The Wheel of Abuse."

The buy-back

Some people call this the "normal" phase or even the "honeymoon period," but in an abusive relationship, nothing is ever really normal, and any honeymoon feeling is a deception. "Buy-back" names what the abuser is doing: trying to manipulatively buy back, through apparent peace and pleasantness, the affection and loyalty of the one he seeks to control. When it suits his purposes, he can pretend to be quite caring, even loving. The buy-back phase will give the victim false hopes that things are better now, that he really does love her, that he has truly changed. But like almost everything the abuser does, this is ultimately all for himself.

The buildup

In this phase, tension builds. The abuser begins to see everything his victim does as a challenge to his power and authority. He begins to plan how he will deliver his next explosion of abuse to bring her back under his control.

The setup

The abuser looks for ways to set up his victim, an excuse to strike. Like an evil dictator looking for an excuse to start a war, he may create the incident, using one of the tactics described in the next chapter. Because his ultimate desire is to exercise control, the victim will fail in all her attempts to please him.

---

[36] Lundy Bancroft, *Why Does He Do That? Inside the Minds of Angry and Controlling Men* (Berkley Books, 2003), p 147.

> *My mom used to tell me, "Don't push his buttons!" She didn't understand that he was all buttons.*

The blowup

The abuser now launches his all-out attack in one of several ways. His goals will be to intimidate the victim to remain small and in her place of subjection and servitude, and to convince her that she is entirely at fault for his abuse.

The cover-up

An abuser at this stage may put on displays of guilt and remorse.[37] He may feign empathy, shame, and sorrow for his wrongdoing. He may express his love for his victim in what appears at first to be a very genuine way. But it is a sham, often simply mimicked and mirrored from outward behavior that he has observed in others. One giveaway is that there will almost always be some form of excuse and blame directed toward someone else, usually his victim.

The buy-back

The abuser will cycle back to the beginning, to what some call the "normal" phase, only to repeat the cycle over and over again. But remember, what some call "normal" is really manipulation in disguise, or "buy-back." Great damage can be done to victims during this stage, as it increases the victim's confusion.

Just remember, in every phase of this abuse cycle, abuse is operating.

No matter how contrite or charming the abuser might appear in various phases of the cycle, inevitably the overt abuse will resume. When a victim sees that the "calms" between overtly abusive periods are decreasing and the directly abusive acts are intensifying, she should take this as a warning sign that she is in imminent danger.

---

[37] Some abusers skip the guilt and remorse phase altogether.

With a void of conscience, with a mindset of entitlement, with important characteristics lacking, and with the ability to wear a respectable mask, the abuser is clearly a dangerous person. In order to obtain and maintain the power and control that he craves, he will use specific tactics as his wicked and deceitful weapons, standard issue equipment in the dark world of abuse.

After reading our description of the tactics explained in the next two chapters, many victims have told us, "I can't believe it! Those are precisely the things he does to me. Do these guys all study at the same wicked school?"

Largely, the answer to that question is yes. They do indeed all have the same Instructor. Jesus said to the hypocritical abusers of His day:

> *You are of your father the devil,*
>   *and your will is to do your father's desires.*
> *He was a murderer from the beginning,*
>   *and has nothing to do with the truth,*
>   *because there is no truth in him.*
> *When he lies, he speaks out of his own character,*
>   *for he is a liar and the father of lies.*[38]

---

[38] John 8:44.

CHAPTER 3

Manipulating Reality

But we have renounced disgraceful, underhanded ways. We refuse to practice cunning or to tamper with God's word, but by the open statement of the truth we would commend ourselves to everyone's conscience in the sight of God.[39]

The favorite weapons of most abusers are psychological or emotional abuse tactics. Victims can attest that these non-physical weapons have been more damaging than physical assault, even when the abuser has "never laid a hand on her."

Emotional abuse systematically degrades, diminishes, and can eventually destroy the personhood of the abused. Most people describe emotional abuse as being far more painful and traumatic than physical abuse. One only has to read reports of prisoners of war to begin to understand the traumatic effects of psychological warfare using emotionally abusive tactics—and this is when the behavior is perpetrated by one's enemy. When the abusive behavior is perpetrated by someone who promises to love and cherish you, it is even more devastating and destructive.[40]

---

[39] II Corinthians 4:2.

[40] Leslie Vernick, *The Emotionally Destructive Marriage: How to Find Your Voice and Reclaim Your Hope* (The Crown Publishing Group, 2013), p 11.

Crazy-making schemes

Gaslighting

In the 1944 movie *Gaslight*, the husband of the main character nearly succeeds in driving his wife crazy. "Gaslighting" eventually came to refer to purposeful efforts to cause a person to doubt her own senses. Another way to refer to it is *crazy making*. Martha Stout describes how effective this tool is even in the broader relationships of the abuser.

> Over the years, listening to hundreds of patients who have been targeted by sociopaths, I have learned that within an organization or a community, in the event that a sociopath is finally revealed to all and sundry, it is not unusual to find that several people suspected all along, each one independently, each one in silence. Each one felt gaslighted, and so each one kept her crazy-sounding secret to herself.[41]

Many if not most abusers play multiple roles. The abuser can turn in moments from the attacker to the victim. His voice can morph in moments from charming, thoughtful kindness into piercing, chilling sarcasm. He may praise his victim for the meal she fixed, and then the next month rage about the very same meal. He may express syrupy romance to her one day, and the next day tell her she's a sorry excuse for a human being. He might cruelly victimize her and then suddenly say, "Hey, let's go out! Put on something pretty and we'll go have a great time!" His unpredictability keeps his victim confused, and confused people are much easier to control.

> *One day he would flaunt his adultery in my face and effectively rub my nose in the dirt with the heel of his shoe, telling me this was my fault and that he didn't regret the affair, and the next day he would cry that he loved me and didn't want to lose me. My whole life and identity had been wrapped up in him for so long that on some level I believed that I did need to be ashamed.*

---

[41] Stout, *The Sociopath Next Door*, p 95.

Another abuse survivor describes how her abuser played with her mind.

> *During my fourteen-year marriage, my husband was a serial cheater. In his quest to hook a new victim, he would pursue and date her like the beginning of any relationship. They would go out for drinks, see a movie, try a restaurant, etc. I can't tell you how many times, in our day-to-day life, when we would drive by said restaurant or see a movie listing, he would insist we had eaten there or seen that specific movie. I would argue vehemently with him, only to have him lash out and tell me how crazy I was, how bad my memory was getting, and how hurt he was that I didn't remember these events. I always walked away feeling confused and angry—angry that he could insist we had been there when we really hadn't, and confused, because what if we had? And what's worse, my family always said what a good memory I had, and now I doubted it.*

We all know that it is much easier to physically manipulate a person, as wrestlers do in a wrestling match, if we can first get them off balance. Abusers know this in the psychological realm, so they work to keep their victim in a continual state of uncertainty and imbalance, always trying to prepare for what he will say or do next. Will he smile or rage? What position will he take on some subject? What will he demand of us today?

This can happen in the workplace too. The employees come to the workday with an orderly and logical plan, but then the boss shows up, suddenly commanding a surprise agenda. He orders the employees to make it happen, ignoring the chaos he has created. The next day, the boss may be in a rage demanding to know why the original plan the employees were all set to carry out had not been completed.

An abuser will cause similar chaos in his home, insuring that he remain the center of everyone's world. His victims become trained to understand that they won't know where he's going unless he chooses to tell them, when he'll be back until he arrives, or what he's planning until he announces it.

> *I can recall a time when he was upset and we tried to just go about our day without catering to his anger. He finally went outside and set the yard on fire on a windy day, so we all had to run around and help him put it out so our house didn't burn down. One time he didn't like something I said at Bible study, so he stopped several miles from our rural home and kicked me out of the car in a snowstorm. He would also drive erratically when he was angry, even going off the road, in order to make me stop addressing concerns he no longer wanted to hear about.*

Besides keeping the focus on him, this planned chaos results in victims who are easier to manipulate, allowing the abuser to maintain his power and control. In such an environment of doubt, family members may even accuse one another, while the source of the problem—the abuser—sits back and watches.

> *He told his son that he was hard on him because if he wasn't, I would make him kick his son out. He blamed me for the abuse and caused his son to hate me.*

Victims who have been free from their abuser for a while can usually describe the atmosphere of chaos and confusion, but early on in the abuse, they often can't even articulate it. Dealing with abusers on a day-to-day basis will leave the victims reeling, as they never know what to expect from him from one day to the next.

> *Yes, the violence and anger in our home had been traumatizing, but living in constant chaos has caused so much long term anxiety and unsettled feelings that still continue.*

Changing the rules

Abusers often use the tactic of changing plans and then telling everyone except their victim. This will serve to make the victim appear to others as if she is mentally unstable or just stupid, not to be trusted or believed.[42]

---

[42] Johnson, *Physical Abusers and Sexual Offenders,* Locations 390-400, Kindle edition.

But even more, the abuser changes the rules. As the abuser changes the rules that his victims are to follow, he will provide himself with ample opportunities to move through the cycle of abuse and plenty of excuses to overtly abuse.

> On his way out the door, he bored his eyes into me, his voice vile with contempt. "You're an embarrassment," he sneered. "I can't stand to be seen with you in public with those ugly clothes you wear."
>
> I was speechless. Because the crazy thing was, he was the one who'd made the rules about how we were to dress. He'd forbidden us to wear prints or pretty colors, saying that they would make us too outwardly attractive. He vehemently proclaimed it immodest to wear anything that would reveal our shape. For years we'd ended up making all our clothes because that was the only way we could come up with ones that would pass the test.
>
> And yet, that morning, somehow all of it had vanished into thin air with no explanation whatsoever, as if he'd never had responsibility or convictions in the matter at all. He handed me fifty dollars and an ultimatum—come up with a whole new wardrobe by the time he got home from work that afternoon.

An abuser can change the rules about something as simple as how the dishcloth should be folded or exactly how full the sugar bowl should be.

> Living off the grid, farming, homesteading, and homeschooling, we were never able to wring enough time out of the day to accomplish all that needed to be done—no matter how hard we worked or how late we stayed up. But when Mom went to Dad for help, he declared that the only reason we had a problem was because we were undisciplined and poor stewards of the time God had entrusted to us.
>
> His solution was to institute a new rule. At that time we were only eating two meals a day—which from now on were to be served at 9 am and 2 pm sharp. Whichever of us girls was responsible for cooking that day would be required to have everything completely ready by then. Not only did we have to have all the food prepared and served and the table set to the nines including salt, pepper, napkins, and anything else anyone might conceivably want with that meal, but we also needed to have the rest of the family found and called in from the fields, washed, and sitting quietly in

their seats. And, hardest of all, we also had to make sure everyone's work scheduled to be done by that time of the day was finished, too—farm chores done, dishes and laundry caught up, firewood brought in, daily project assignments done, etc. If we were even one second late with any aspect—he made this very clear—we would cause our family to lose the privilege of eating that meal.

We tried—very hard. Sometimes we were able to pull it off. But plenty of times we simply couldn't. With a large family on a farm, unexpected things always came up and threw off even the best plans. And then too, sometimes we just missed something by mistake. Once, my sister had made a particularly nice dinner. She managed to get everything done in the nick of time, only to realize she'd neglected to bring the asparagus over from the stove. By the time she grabbed it, Dad pronounced us late. It was only a matter of seconds—less than a minute for sure—but the clock had struck, and there was no dinner for us that day.

Unknowable

It was approximately two years prior to my abuser's desertion that he told me he did not love me anymore. His reason was I could not have possibly been the person God had promised him. He kept a record of how I had disappointed him. He told me that he thought he had loved me as Christ loved the church.

I was in such a fog and brainwashed to believe everything he said that I told him tearfully that I agreed with him—he was a wonderful husband and I didn't deserve him. Until he left, I would constantly ask for his forgiveness to be sure everything was right between us. Sometimes after I had gone to bed when he was still awake, I would beg his forgiveness in case I had done anything wrong that day. He told me he "forgave" me and to let it go, but he did not let it go.

When my attorney added adultery as an addendum to the divorce proceedings, his attorney responded by accusing me of abuse. The judge didn't believe it one bit, but I was heartbroken to think he would accuse me of this. I prayed earnestly and racked my brain to see if this was true.

Abuse victims often talk about living in a fog, without the clarity of vision to perceive the truth about their abuser and his tactics. Abusers promote this lack of clarity because they want to remain unknown—a mystery.

In order to make himself unreachable and unknowable, an abuser will often withdraw in sullen silence, refusing to speak at all. He may make himself hard to find or hard to reach. He may "look through" the victim without a word. He may speak unfinished sentences that leave the victim struggling to figure out how to complete the thought. He may speak half-truths or use statements that are ambiguous, so that the victim is left trying to understand what he meant.[43]

Turning reality on its head

Storytelling

For wicked and deceitful mouths are opened against me,
  speaking against me with lying tongues.[44]

Because of the abuser's lack of conscience and mindset of entitlement, he can spin his stories with remarkable certainty in whatever ways he needs to in order to achieve his desired goals. If he meets some objection to the logic of what he is saying, he can simply change the story. "She came outside and stood behind me nagging me, so I just threw that tool over my shoulder in disgust. She stepped to one side on purpose so it would hit her in the face." His confidence and unblinking certainty in describing the scene, the tool itself, and her devious behavior can make a bizarre story sound convincing.

An abuser might also use the passive voice and other language that indicates that he was being acted upon by forces beyond his control. "We *got* into an argument and *she made me* so angry the lamp *got broken.* She provoked me so much that *the words just came out. When she looked at me that way,* my fist just went into her face."

The victim may have personally witnessed the abuser say or do something incriminating, but he will call her crazy, claiming that he never said or did such a thing. She may also find herself faced with some

---

[43] Bancroft, *Why Does He Do That?* pp 3-20.
[44] Psalm 109:2.

story the abuser claims took place that she doesn't remember at all. Still, he is so confident that she may often begin to doubt her own memory and perceptions, her own senses and conclusions.[45] A person who no longer fully trusts in what her senses tell her is a person who is very easy to control.

> *Soon after we separated I discovered my abuser had copied all my current emails on my computer when he came to pick up the kids for a visit. After that he was no longer allowed in the house. A few months later he barged into my house without permission, and I called 911. That night he emailed me, blaming me and saying he had done it respectfully (he had shouted "coming in"). Two days later he said that he saw me "change" and "act" like I was threatened before I called 911. (I was in utter fear—he outweighs me by 150 pounds easily.)*
>
> *One week later these were his words about what happened (and they were sent to numerous people on email, so no expectation of privacy: according to him, I set up the whole incident, manipulating him into coming into my house so I could call 911 and "entrap" him): "<u>About coming into the house</u>: Sunday scared the daylights out of me and has given me concerns about entrapment, so I won't be coming into the house alone and when possible will have a police officer or a witness with me for my protection."*

Morphing the victim's words

> *Now the serpent was more crafty than any other beast of the field that the LORD God had made. He said to the woman, "Did God actually say, 'You shall not eat of any tree in the garden?'"*[46]

Satan's goal in the garden was to accuse God, and he made this accusation by subtly twisting what God had really said. He made the Lord out to be too "restrictive" by adding the little word "any" and doing so in question form. Abusers, being the sons of the devil that they are, betray their diabolical DNA by twisting their victim's words and motives to make them look like fools, or crazy, or even abusive. A victim can

---

[45] Bancroft, *Why Does He Do That?* Chapter 6.
[46] Genesis 3:1.

often come away from a conversation with an abuser saying, "Did I really say that? Is that what I really meant?"

> *We were in bed for the night, and my husband tried to "start something" not long after he had mistreated me throughout the day. I said, "I don't want to do that tonight. I have a hard time doing that with how you've treated me today."*
>
> *He said, "You know, withholding sex as punishment is wrong."*
>
> *I said, "That's not what I'm doing."*
>
> *He said, "Well then, what do you call it?"*
>
> *I said, "Being very hurt by your treatment and not willing to make myself vulnerable to you in that way right now."*
>
> *To which he responded, "Right. Like I said. Withholding sex as punishment."*

Playing the victim

Disturbed characters are good at portraying themselves as the victims of injustice. . . . It's a sly tool to make someone who wants to confront them appear insensitive and heartless. A most egregious example of this remains embedded in my memory to this day. I was interviewing a prisoner who vigorously denied the crime for which he had most recently been convicted. He blamed "the system" for arresting him out of prejudice, but readily admitted a long history of antisocial conduct that included a murder in which he fully participated, but for which he was never convicted. He described a vicious assault in which he and two accomplices bludgeoned a man to death. Yet he complained, "I have to live with the image of that horrible event in my mind for the rest of my life."[47]

Sociopaths, narcissists, and abusers love to be pitied. An abused spouse will regularly hear about all the ways others have mistreated her abuser. The victim stories can be from work . . .

---

[47] Simon, *Character Disturbance,* Location 1867-1872, Kindle edition.

> *For 25 years I listened as he described how he was always the victim of his boss at work. Over and over he changed jobs because they didn't understand him, wouldn't implement his wonderful ideas, had personality clashes, didn't pay enough, passed him over for promotion, just seemed to not like him. At first I was sympathetic, but as it happened repeatedly I began to wonder why there was such a long string of bad bosses in his life. Although deep in the fog, I began to wonder when my turn would come.*

or from childhood. . . .

> *There was no denying that my husband was abused by his mother as a child—she was a cruel person. He always compared me to his mother when I would try to defend myself. Suddenly he was that scared hurt little boy again and I needed to protect him. I would excuse his behavior and ill treatment of me and even feel guilty for having been hurt by his actions. But then he began to hurt our children, and I realized that he was no longer that hurt little boy. And I wasn't his mother—I was theirs! And my kids needed me to protect them.*

Because of the abuser's absence of conscience, mindset of justification, and double standard, he sees no problem with attacking his victim verbally or even physically. But if his victim tries to defend herself, he will suddenly become the victim, a transformation that he can pull off in the blink of an eye.

> *The tension and control became unbearable, and I left him, desperate to protect myself and our two small children. He immediately became the contrite husband, the weeping husband, the man who had no idea that he had wounded me. He lost his faith in God one moment, and had a spiritual epiphany the next. He sent out a letter to multiple people, telling them of my childhood abuse and the details of our marital breakdown and just how sorry he was. He flipped into an aggressive and volatile state at other times, harassing me and my family incessantly. He made a public scene in the church I considered my refuge, and sent Christians my way to talk some sense into me. When that failed, he sent these good Christian folk to my friends in the hopes that someone could arrange a talk that would change my mind. He filed for sole custody of the children (unsuccessfully) and tried to prevent them from seeing a counselor. He told*

> *them to forget their mother, that I was nothing special. Throughout it all, he considered himself the sole victim and continues to do so.*

A common tactic of an abuser is accusing his victim of trying to manipulate him, when she does something such as laying a book on her night stand about praying for your husband. A victim with a strong conscience (as most victims are) will take this accusation to heart and question herself. But who is really the manipulative one?

"Psychological manipulation can be defined as the exercise of undue influence through mental distortion and emotional exploitation, with the intention to seize power, control, benefits, and privileges at the victim's expense."[48]

None of these criteria are met by a victim who lets her abuser know that she is praying for him to change. Psychological manipulation is the work of the abuser. Not the victim.

Using the victim's conscience against her

Because the victim has a conscience and the ability to empathize, the abuser will often use his skill at twisting the truth and rewriting history to confuse the victim to the point that she will think that she should apologize. Maybe, she thinks, she really was too harsh and judgmental.

He may put on a very convincing display of miserable tears, insisting that his victim pity and forgive him, especially when he suspects that she may escape. He may threaten or attempt suicide to evoke pity. He may make a show of conversion or recommitment to Christ and/or counseling, especially if she has recently escaped from him. But despite this show, he will still minimize his responsibility and still subtly make it look like his victim is at fault.[49]

---

[48]Preston Ni, MSBA, "How to Spot and Stop Manipulators: 8 tips for keeping them at a distance, or breaking free," *Psychology Today*, Jun 1, 2014, accessed via https://www.psychologytoday.com/blog/communication-success/201406/how-spot-and-stop-manipulators

[49]Barbara Roberts, *Not Under Bondage: Biblical Divorce for Abuse, Adultery, and Desertion* (Maschil Press, 2008), p 25.

All of this, of course, is designed to attack the victim's conscience, load her down with a false conviction of guilt, until a remarkable outcome is accomplished—the victim apologizes to the abuser! (Abuse victims are often characterized by an unusual frequency of the phrase "I'm sorry.")

Abusers tend to look for victims with healthy consciences, even overactive ones, victims who are willing to seek their own hearts for sin, again and again. Abusers will use this sometimes overactive conscience to their advantage, weighing their victims down with false guilt in order to control them.

Showing his superiority

Imposing his double standard

The abuser won't allow his victim to even consider touching anything that belongs to him, but he'll dispose of his victim's personal property as he sees fit.

> He had his own bedroom in the house with a key that I wasn't allowed to have. But he took my diaries—even the ones from before I met him—and read them and even showed them to other people to mock me.

When he is sick, he'll insist that he get the best of care, but he will mock her or the children for an illness. He can treat the children very harshly, calling it justified, deserved discipline, but if she yells at them, he calls her a terrible parent. He can enjoy a laugh at the expense of someone else, but if his victims are laughing together over something that he is not a part of, it can send him into a rage.

> I couldn't even go out for a cup of coffee with my mom because he said that's what women did to pick up men. Meanwhile, he was going to breakfast every morning with his friends.

True happiness in the home of an abuser is not allowed.

He bought me a new car, but I wasn't allowed to drive it anywhere without his permission. I wasn't allowed to shop for myself without his presence, which usually meant that I didn't need anything unless he determined that I needed it. He kept track of the mileage on my car. He, on the other hand, had access to several vehicles that belonged only to him and had the freedom to come and go as he pleased without accountability.

Minimizing his own wrongdoing

In I Samuel 15:13-15, King Saul told Samuel that he had kept the commandment of the Lord, in spite of the fact that he had not. A classic minimizer of his own grievous sin (as well as a blamer), Saul represented his own faults as miniscule. Because the abuser sees his world through his own special set of lenses, this is what he does, even while he sees the faults of others as mammoth.

> The disordered character uses the tactic of minimizing primarily to manipulate others into thinking he's not such a bad person. But minimizing serious transgressions is also the way the disturbed character lies to himself about the full extent of his character deficiencies and behavioral problems.[50]

Seeing all of life as a competition

> [W]hen emotional attachment and conscience are missing . . . life is reduced to a contest, and other human beings seem to be nothing more than game pieces, to be moved about, used as shields, or ejected. . . . Controlling others—winning—is more compelling than anything (or anyone) else.[51]

The abuser's do-or-die sense of competition can come through in a variety of ways, but one of them is in marriage counseling. If the counselor unwisely decides to counsel the couple together, then almost anything the victim shares in that setting will later be used against her. With no desire for real peace in the relationship, the abuser views marriage counseling as a competition to be won.

---

[50]Simon, *Character Disturbance*, Locations 1815-1821, Kindle edition.

[51]Stout, *The Sociopath Next Door*, pp 46-47.

"I have really been in denial about my violence," [Quentin] told the therapist, "and I haven't been facing how badly it has been affecting Irene." The therapist felt that a crucial barrier to progress had been overcome. "Now," he declared, "I think your couples work can begin to yield results for you."

On the drive home from the session, Quentin kept one hand on the steering wheel. In the other hand he clutched a large handful of Irene's hair as he repeatedly slammed her head into the dashboard, screaming, "I told you to never f**ing talk to anyone about that, you b**! You promised me! You're a f**ing liar!" and similar insults in a nonstop rant. After hearing Irene's account, I was careful to never again underestimate the risk to an abused woman of conjoint therapy.[52]

If his victim escapes, the abuser will also see the entire justice system as a competition to be won. This "legal bullying" can be done in regard to custody of the children, whom he does not love but considers to be his property.[53]

An abuser may violate legitimate laws with no pang of conscience because he believes that he is above the law and thinks "it's stupid." One common example is challenging the rules of the road, which can lead to road rage and other dangerous driving that can put his life and the lives of others in danger.

> Safety seemed to be of no concern to him. He would purposely drive in the middle of the road, straddling the yellow line, when he thought he could get away with it. Despite the fact that he regularly fell asleep at the wheel, he absolutely refused to let anyone else drive. Whoever was riding in the front seat had to always be ready to grab the steering wheel to keep the vehicle from crashing.

Even when arrested, an abuser will regard the whole episode as ridiculous and unfair, as if the system is just out to get him.

---

[52]Bancroft, *Why Does He Do That?* p 354.

[53]More about abuse through the legal system is considered in Chapter 9.

Once, on the way home from church, his driving was so erratic that the car behind us flagged us down. The guy came up to the driver's side window and thoroughly lambasted him for so recklessly endangering his family's lives, especially with children in the car. It made quite an impression on me that a total stranger had noticed and cared enough to do something, but none of it seemed to faze him at all. He just used it as an object lesson to us of the sinful way that The World acted.

One way outsiders can be alerted to the possibility that a person may be a domestic abuser is in his unwillingness to take a stance as a listener and learner. Instead, not only does the typical abuser have an opinion on almost every subject, but he expresses it as if it is fact. The "Christian" abuser may show up in church as one who always knows better than the Bible study teacher.

"When Mr. Right decides to take control of a conversation, he switches into his Voice of Truth, giving the definitive pronouncement on what is the correct answer or the proper outlook. Abuse counselors call this tactic defining reality.*"*[54]

The boredom of royalty

A conscience-less person with a mindset of entitlement, control, and justification will easily become bored with his life. Refusing to take on responsibility for that with which he has been entrusted leads to a life of monochromatic monotony. Responsible stewardship is just too boring, even if it means his family suffers from lack. The abuser must move on for his next adventure, seeking the fulfillment that he will never find. Care of the mundane is beneath him.

Because the abuser believes that nothing is ever his fault, he looks to those around him for the reason for his boredom and the solution for the monotony. "You're no fun anymore!"

[54]Bancroft, *Why Does He Do That?* p 82.

> *Six weeks after the birth of our child, I started to hemorrhage and was rushed to the hospital. The loss of blood, coupled with my birth injuries, made recovery difficult. Soon after, I found my husband using pornography. This discovery, and his scathing anger, provoked flashbacks of the violent sexual abuse and exposure to pornography in my early childhood. Rather than empathizing with me in my distress, however, he blamed me for his addiction—an addiction that had started more than ten years before we met. He blamed my shoddy housekeeping, my reluctance to entertain guests during my challenging pregnancy, and the fact that I had not spared him from being "bored." Some close Christian friends, hoping to salvage our marriage, showed me how to better organize the refrigerator.*

"Such a nice man"

> *These . . . wicked assailants . . . constantly cloak their evil ways from being seen from the outside. And oh, they always know what Bible verses to say, what soft words to say, what charm to spring out to those who are called to investigate. People say he is the best neighbor and first to volunteer to help! He gets away with EVERYTHING. And I am left to raise the children with nothing from him but grief and fear.*

We are seduced . . . by the acting skills of the sociopath. Since the scaffolding of a life without conscience is deception and illusion, intelligent sociopaths often become proficient at acting, and even at some of the particular techniques employed by professional actors. Paradoxically, the visible signs of emotion at will can become second nature to the cold-blooded—the appearance of intense interest in another person's problems or enthusiasms, chest-thumping patriotism, righteous indignation, blushing modesty, weepy sadness. Crocodile tears at will are a sociopathic trademark.[55]

"Crocodile tears at will are a sociopathic trademark."
–Martha Stout

---

[55]Stout, *The Sociopath Next Door,* p 91.

The charmer

For there is no truth in their mouth;
their inmost self is destruction;
their throat is an open grave;
they flatter with their tongue.[56]

The word "charm" has a magical connotation. It is almost synonymous with "magic spell." Many abusers can be exceedingly charming, so much so in fact it is as if they have the power to cast that magic spell on anyone they desire to control. And they are good at it.

> *Charming is the first word people would use to describe my emotionally abusive ex-husband. He fairly oozed charm and knew how to use it. He had a way of finding out a person's likes and dislikes and would use that information to ingratiate himself with them. When we met, he used that charm on me. He told me this wonderful story of God promising him a special marriage relationship when he was a child through direct revelation. It was hard to resist the idea that I was his wife promised from God.*
>
> *But his charm could be turned on and off like a switch. When I didn't live up to his expectations, he used his charm as a means to hurt me. He would make a point to be as nice as he could be to our friends when we were together and ice cold toward me in private. When I objected, he accused me of not letting him freely express himself.*
>
> *But if there was something he wanted, the charm turned back on, and I succumbed. I felt like the family dog who was so starved for affection that it would take a pat on the head even if it had been kicked the previous day.*

It isn't at all unusual for the abuser to show "kindnesses" to his victim as part of the disorientation process during the buy-back phase of the cycle of abuse. Overt kindness, as well as simply relief from the abuse, can serve to arouse a new hope in the victim that the abuse may be coming to an end or maybe the counseling is really working.

---

[56] Psalm 5:9.

Things had gotten extremely bad—so bad, in fact, that the pastor reluctantly advised us to consider a temporary separation until we could work things out. But when I tried, he turned into a raging monster and went on a rampage, threatening every evil thing he could think of.

The next day after church he was strangely subdued. He told me that the sermon had spoken to him and he intended to do better. This changed things—the pastor had only said to separate till things got worked out. So I stayed.

I honestly didn't know if it was real. He'd done it so many times—he would drip with sweetness for a while and then go back to being mean. But this time . . . something felt different. Genuine. He was gentle. Caring. Kind and patient and full of grace. For the first time in a long time, it felt safe to breathe. And after two months—longer than it had ever lasted before—I began to let myself believe it might be real.

It was only a few weeks later that the whole charade ripped open. He drove in one night and immediately flew into a raging fury over some little bit of nothing. The children and I were wicked and rebellious and out of control—and had been for months, he said. He'd been foolish to let himself be swayed by people who tried to convince him to let up on us. As our husband and father he had a responsibility before God to keep us in line, and he'd been wrong to sit by and let us get away with murder. He'd been trying to keep his mouth shut, but we just kept getting worse and worse, and he refused to ignore our defiance any longer, no matter who told him otherwise.

Gathering allies

Like glaze covering an earthen vessel are fervent lips with an evil heart. . . .
when he speaks graciously, believe him not,
for there are seven abominations in his heart;
though his hatred be covered with deception,
his wickedness will be exposed in the assembly. . . .
A lying tongue hates its victims, and a flattering mouth works ruin.[57]

One of the abuser's most formidable weapons is his ability to win over all the victim's relational connections. The abuser knows that

---

Christians want to help the weak, so his goal is for people to perceive him as the victim. He will turn reality on its head to convince her relatives, friends, co-workers, church elders, and even children that *she* is the real culprit in their marriage difficulties.

The chief reason victims are disregarded when they report their abuse is that others firmly believe the abuser's unholy charade of righteousness, the wolf's covering of wool.

> *According to our son, my husband told a woman he barely knew in the middle of a Wal-Mart aisle that I was "divorcing him" and to please "pray for my wife's salvation." Of course they wouldn't feel so sorry for him if he disclosed the truth: he abused his wife and children, he forged an addiction to pornography off and on for our entire marriage, he believes everything is ok as long as he says the words "I'm sorry," and the list goes on. Yes, I did file, but I did not annihilate our wedding vows, and I most certainly am a believer and follower of Jesus Christ.*

The local church is sadly, one of the best places for abusers to gather allies, and they know it. Even all varieties of legal and social workers can become their pawns to be used against the victim.

> *I told my story of abuse and mental torture—at the hands of my well-known husband—to the director at the domestic violence shelter. I didn't know that the director was my husband's graduate psychology student, or that she was going to call him immediately after I left. I didn't know that he was carefully circulating a story around town that I had a personality disorder and therefore made up stories about abuse. He was able to convince professionals that I was hitting myself for attention. He had crafted this tale because, unknown to me, he knew that someday I'd tell, and he laid the groundwork to demolish my credibility before I ever opened my mouth.*
>
> *When he came home, he told me with a smirk and a laugh, "I know where you were today. That director is my graduate student, and she called me and said, 'your wife was here, but don't worry we don't believe her, because we know about her.'" The workers at the shelter actually had never met me before, so the only way they "knew" all about me was based on the word of a monstrous abuser.*

But the Bible has the last word on the façade of the abuser who charms:

For such men are false apostles, deceitful workmen,

disguising themselves as apostles of Christ.

And no wonder,

for even Satan disguises himself as an angel of light.

So it is no surprise if his servants, also,

disguise themselves as servants of righteousness.[58]

---

[58] II Corinthians 11:13-15.

CHAPTER 4

Weapons of Degradation and Terror

Discretion will watch over you, understanding will guard you,
delivering you from the way of evil, from men of perverted speech,
who forsake the paths of uprightness to walk in the ways of darkness,
who rejoice in doing evil and delight in the perverseness of evil,
men whose paths are crooked, and who are devious in their ways.[59]

I don't think that the church would fall into such uncertainty if we were discussing the psychological torture of political prisoners and its morality. There are myriad resources and papers from various humanitarian and human rights organizations that validate the reality of psychological torture and its effect on the brain.

Interestingly enough, a frightening similarity can be seen between "official" torture and the tactics of an abuser. This is the disgusting beauty of it for abusers with upstanding public reputations—absolute deniability. And a deniability often endorsed by church officials, which leads to the syllogistic conclusion that the wife is mentally ill or just a liar.

Emotional abuse can take so many different forms that those who have never experienced it need instruction before they can even begin to understand it. Aside from outright verbal and physical assault, which is

---

[59] Proverbs 2:11-15.

at least more obvious, the abuser can abuse in many ways that the victim may find nearly impossible to explain. The crazy-making described in the previous chapter can be seamlessly integrated with the forms of abuse described in this chapter, so that by the time the victim finally escapes for her life, when she faces the common question "Why didn't you leave sooner?" she'll often find herself unable to answer it.

Degrading the victim

Objectification and jealousy

The wicked plots against the righteous and gnashes his teeth at him.[60]

Human traffickers throughout the world see children as objects to be bought and sold and possessed for the sex or labor or experimentation they can be used for. Just as these traffickers speak of children as commodities to be exchanged, so the domestic abuser speaks of his victim in degrading or even non-human terms. The term often used for this attitude is *objectification*: regarding a person as an object, a tool, or an extension of himself.

Ownership and possession explain why abusers often feel intense jealousy regarding their victims. An abuser won't tolerate what "belongs" to him even having conversations with others. He'll portray his intense, completely unreasonable jealousy as passionate love. But in reality it is not about love but about possession.[61]

> He made me feel like . . . no one else could ever love me. I should be grateful to him. He told me several times that he was the only one who would put up with me—I just annoyed everyone.

---

[60] Psalm 37:12.

[61] See Bancroft, *Why Does He Do That?* pp 317-319. Bancroft explains through allegory how boys are trained to view women as pieces of property to be possessed. Also see Barbara Roberts' article, "Still Married in the Sight of God," http://notunderbondage.com/pages/still-married-in-the-sight-of-god-how-this-expression-has-been-used-in-christendom. That slogan is used as spiritual abuse to enforce the abuser's ownership of his wife.

Treating her like a servant and a child

The domestic abuser views his victim as his ignorant servant. In his mind, it is the job of his victim to clean up after him and keep him happy. Even if she has been ill or has just come home from the hospital after giving birth, he will often insist that she get back to the housework, wait on him, and give him sex.

The television and computer are often under the complete control of the abuser. Sometimes he even hides the remote or mouse when he's gone. He may restrict his victim's travel, watching the odometer of the car to make sure she didn't drive farther than to the permitted destination and back. If she has, she will be grilled, yelled at, and punished.

Instead of being a lifeline to the outside world, a victim's cell phone can become one more means of isolation and control. The abuser will manipulate and control through text messages, sometimes dozens or scores every day, demanding to know where she is and what she is doing. He can even put a tracking device on her cell phone.

The abuser's victim is often highly restricted in her use of money. The family of an abuser may live in poverty because of his unwise spending or refusal to work. He may sabotage his victim's efforts to operate a home business for supplemental income.

> I was required to hand over every receipt for every single purchase, but once again, that meant I couldn't buy anything without his permission even though I had a job and paid all the household bills and expenses. He said that his money needed to go towards building our business and a retirement fund, but I noticed that he had plenty of money to buy whatever he wanted, including, cars, motorcycles, guns, trips with the guys, and clothes. Clothes were something that I apparently didn't need. He would bring home new clothes for himself and parade them for me to admire. If I bought new clothes, he would become very angry and make me feel guilty for spending money. I lived like a penniless beggar.

The abuser, considering himself superior to his victim, does not value her thoughts and input, believing that she should see things as he does. Not only is she not permitted to make independent plans, but she becomes less and less free to even have her own thoughts. All too often, the abuser manages to replace God. As one victim said, "He determined the holiness of my dedication to God." The abuser instructs the victim in her "duty," telling her not only what she should do, but even what she should think.

> There was never space to actually discuss something with my husband. He would state his opinion on a situation and ask what I thought. But when I would genuinely offer my perspective, he'd lash out at me. It became apparent that, no matter the subject, he considered his opinion to be the only right—and therefore Godly—one, and the fact that I didn't automatically validate it was proof I wasn't submitted to him or to God.
>
> As time went on, it got to the point where he would quiz me about my opinion on a subject without first sharing his viewpoint. It was a kind of test—if my thoughts ended up mirroring his, then I would "pass." If they differed (and since he hadn't yet told me what he thought, I could only guess what he was going to consider the "right" answer), then I obviously wasn't right with the Lord. If I was truly in fellowship with God, he reminded me, God would have put in my heart the same perspective He'd already revealed to him as my husband.

Blaming and accusing

To an abuser, the majority of the blame for any wrongdoing always rests with a source outside himself, often the victim. Even hard evidence of wrongdoing will not turn most abusers to admission of guilt. The intensity of the abuser's blame-shifting can be intimidating, like a thick concrete wall.[62]

> I began seeing a decades-long pattern of behavior that included serious verbal and emotional abuse from my wife. . . . I thought it was my duty to love her like Christ loved the church so I hung in there through it all with that posture as my conviction. I was to be kind to her, patient, and loving, regardless of how she treated me. What I did not understand as I am even now slowly (and I do mean slowly), beginning to realize and being willing to admit was that my wife seems to me to have been dedicated to my

---

[62] Stout, *The Sociopath Next Door*, pp 49-50.

destruction. Frequent undermining, a growing sense that I was dependent on her and that I could not think, making me feel like I could not trust my judgment, complaining about things I would not do to her liking, how I dressed, mannerisms, how I thought, and bringing up past failures and sins that long ago I had asked her forgiveness for, etc.[63]

Many abusers are so masterful at their blame-shifting that the victim can actually begin to think that nothing is really his fault—not their fight, not their lack of funds, not even his adultery. Instead, the victim did this or that—doesn't she remember?—or didn't do what she should have done, so it should be obvious that it's really her fault. As this intense blame-shifting brainwashing continues over time, victims will begin to apologize for incidents in which they were not only innocent, but had been truly victimized.

Revelation 12:10 calls Satan "the accuser of our brothers." Just like their father the devil, abusers love to accuse their victims. While abusive people have dysfunctional or even non-functional consciences, their victims have very active consciences, which the abuser will use to his advantage.

A particularly devious tactic is to accuse the victim of sinful motives behind harmless actions.

Because the victim is already confused and has been taught that her heart is deceitful and desperately wicked,[64] she can begin to second guess her true motives. "Was that what I was really thinking?"

I was looking in the silverware drawer to choose a fork to put in my husband's lunch—one that wouldn't matter too much if it didn't return. He said, "I know what you're doing. You're trying to give me the worst fork in the drawer." His tone was accusatory and demeaning, strongly conveying the message that I was doing something terribly wrong—

---

[63] Though the majority of abusers are men, I do understand that some men are victims of abuse.

[64] This teaching, which the abuser ignores regarding himself, is based on Jeremiah 17:9, which describes the unregenerate human heart.

> certainly refusing to show him the impeccable respect he was due as "king"
> of our family. Clearly, in his mind he was worthy of only the very best
> fork in the drawer—even in his sack lunch.
>
> I thought, "Yes, I guess I am . . ." but felt very confused at the time—was
> this simple, seemingly innocent act of choosing a fork for my husband's
> lunch really the grievous sin against him that he considered it to be? It was
> not until years later (after I had finally separated from him after 25 years
> of abuse) that I was able to process through this event. It was then that I
> realized I would have hunted for the same type of fork if I had been
> packing my own lunch—and that it was a perfectly reasonable thing to do.

The mindset behind an abuser's false accusations of his victim may be related to a dynamic that psychologists call *projection*—attributing one's own undesirable thoughts and attitudes to someone else. [65] For example, because he is out to use people, he proclaims that she is out to use him. If he is unfaithful in his marriage, he claims that she is an adulteress. When he accuses his victim, he is maliciously projecting his own mindset, his own worldview.

The abuser will accuse the victim to others too—her church elders, her boss at work, her family members. One abuser called his wife's work place anonymously and told her boss that she was using drugs and should be drug-tested immediately. If an innocent person is accused often enough, no matter how preposterous the charges, others can begin to believe them. Even she can begin to believe them. Constant attacks constitute one crucial way that abusers garner allies for themselves.

Ridiculing, mocking, assaultive speech

> Do not envy a man of violence and do not choose any of his ways,
> for the devious person is an abomination to the LORD,
> but the upright are in his confidence.
> The LORD's curse is on the house of the wicked,
> but he blesses the dwelling of the righteous.
> Toward the scorners he is scornful, but to the humble he gives favor. [66]

---

[65] Bancroft, *Why Does He Do That?* p 142.
[66] Proverbs 3:31-34.

The tongue of the abuser is one of his primary weapons.

He uses it to change the rules, to declare his expertise, to minimize, to play the victim, to rewrite history, to charm others, to blame, and to accuse. But when the tongue of the abuser turns to ridiculing, mocking, assaultive speech, it is then that it becomes particularly hellish.

Abusive people "shoot" vile epithets at their selected targets like a man shooting a military weapon. He might call his victim a fat cow, an ugly b***h, a whore, or far worse.[67] He might say she is stupid, ignorant, and good for nothing. His barrage can include that she's terrible at cooking, terrible at housekeeping, terrible at sex, terrible at child-raising. If he is speaking "Christian-ese," he might call her a rebellious woman or a Jezebel woman. If he is too self-righteous to use vile terms for human excrement, he might call her a "flush-toilet woman."

> *Mom was naturally animated and vivacious, but Dad strove to systematically grind this out of her. When she'd talk enthusiastically about something, he'd mock her for "running around without any clothes on again." He'd tongue-lash and berate her until she was broken and in tears, even pulling out Scripture to manipulate her own conscience against her, telling her that God commanded her to have a gentle and quiet spirit and that godly women were to be shamefaced and full of sobriety. By then she'd be apologizing and assuring him she did want to learn to do better.*
>
> *Then he would soften his tone and come up with some new rule to help her learn to be more obedient. Once, he implemented a system whereby he would start humming "Blessed Quietness" whenever he heard her starting to get excited about something. Another time he nailed a big ugly "G" and "Q" [for "gentle" and "quiet"] to the kitchen wall so that every time she'd*

---

[67] I reluctantly refrain from directly quoting the graphic language victims are subjected to by their abusers. I say "reluctantly" because while we have the option of avoiding them here, victims do not enjoy that luxury. It seems to me that if we are to truly bear the burdens of the victim, we must not be naïve to anything that they have to suffer. But, as this book is primarily directed toward Christians, I will refrain so as to not put an unnecessary obstacle before anyone in reading this book. Please realize however that the "saintly" Christian man in your church who is, in fact, an abuser, uses horrible, ugly, wicked, and profane language at home to further assault his victim.

> *see them she'd be reminded to control herself. Or he'd even forbid her to*
> *speak out loud for days to help her learn to be quiet.*

Many abuse victims have testified to the sickeningly mocking tone their abuser has used to strip them of their dignity, confidence, joy, and sense of self-worth. Words that assault and tear down the dignity of the victim rob her of her strength to resist him. A person who begins to believe the labels assigned to her by her abuser is a person who is far easier to control.

The abuser may control his language in front of his victim's parents or friends, whom he may suspect of helping her see through the fog. But he may well verbally assault his victim in front of their children in order to undermine her position in the family and her personal dignity. The tactic of shame loves an audience. If he can get his children to laugh at their mother, then not only can they deride her together, but together they can say, "Can't you take a joke?"

Silence and isolation

Many abusive people torment their victims with silence. Victims have testified of their abusers refusing to speak to them for days, without their even understanding what it is they've done to offend them.

> *I was so lonely in my marriage. His favorite tactic was to ignore me, not*
> *talk to me, or touch me. For over a decade we slept in separate rooms. For*
> *over a decade he wouldn't even kiss me. When I was in labor with my*
> *fifth child, he wouldn't even hold my hand during a painful contraction.*
> *At one point I was making a shushing sound to bear through a*
> *contraction, and he thought that I was shushing him. He instantly became*
> *angry (at the time I didn't know why). I reached my hand out to him at*
> *the height of the contraction, but he just stared me down like a worthless*
> *mutt. I remember feeling so alone, I thought the hurt and pain of the*
> *forced solitude would kill me. At times I wished it had.*

Abusers also work to isolate their victim from other people, using ingenious tactics. "Perpetrators of domestic battery demand that their victims prove complete obedience and loyalty by sacrificing all other relationships."[68] All of these tactics have the same purpose and motive—to keep her from making connections with anyone who might encourage her to think for herself or who might help her escape his power and control.

> *Every friend we managed to make, we lost because of him. He'd discover some discrepancy between our doctrinal understanding and theirs and cut off communication in the name of Biblical separation. Other friends drifted away after they got sick of his toxicity—they couldn't stand to see us living in squalor, oppressed by his suffocating tyranny. Another friend decided to stop getting together after she got close enough to decipher his pattern. He'd cut them off soon anyway, she reasoned, and she didn't want her girls to have to go through that. So they slipped away before he could get the satisfaction of forbidding us to see them again.*

The abuser might decide to move often from town to town in order to prevent his victim from developing a support system. He may decide to live the wilderness family life in an isolated location while homeschooling.[69] He may threaten that he can cut her off from all finances at any time. He might prevent his victim from attempting to engage in any activities outside the home.

> *One Sunday afternoon, my daughter worked up the courage to ask him if we could visit a long-time family friend who lived just up the road. She'd recently been widowed, and we wanted to give her a bit of love and encouragement. But my husband lit into us, accusing us of being worldly, discontent, and out of control. "God said women are to be keepers AT HOME," he retorted. "But no, you don't care about obeying Him"—his tone was mocking now—"all you care about is running off to do your own thing whenever you feel like it." That was ridiculous, not to mention a perversion of Scripture and a complete lie. We never ran around doing anything—we'd often go for weeks or months without leaving our property at all. And all we'd wanted to do this time was "visit the . . . widows in their affliction" like it said in James.*

---

[68] Herman, *Trauma and Recovery*, p 76.

[69] I'm not opposed to homeschooling—many of the members of our church home school. But homeschooling has been seen to be an effective means of isolating the victims in cases of abusers who choose the façade of Christianity.

As abuse victims endure abuse over time, their sense of self-worth and confidence deteriorates to become a growing sense of worthlessness and confusion. As confidence decreases and confusion increases, they can begin to fear being with other people and thus self-isolate. Abuse also takes its toll on the victim's physical health, and semi-invalids don't get out much.

Violation of boundaries

To be healthy, functional human beings, each person is entitled to have limits that are respected by others.[70] These boundaries are clearly stated in the last six of the Ten Commandments as one way that we show love for each other.

But an abuser's violation of his victim's boundaries
is so regular and constant that she may lose all sense of
appropriate boundaries.

Besides his words, he will employ other means of boundary violation in order to destroy the dignity and self-worth of his victims. He may violate his children's sense of self-control, for example, by continuing to tickle them after they plead with him to stop. His victim's personal correspondence and private journals will not be respected as private. He'll think nothing of eavesdropping on a private conversation, believing he has the "right" to know what is being discussed. He will violate her privacy in the bathroom. He will violate her body in the bedroom.[71]

> *One Christmas morning, the children were waiting for their father to get up to come out to celebrate the holiday. But he never did. It was past noon, and when I went in the bedroom to see why he wouldn't come out, it was obvious that he was waiting for me, and expected me to "perform" for him, before he was willing to celebrate the holiday with his children. But since I*

---

[70] For a detailed discussion of this important topic, see Henry Cloud and John Townsend, *Boundaries: When to Say Yes, How to Say No to Take Control of Your Life* (Zondervan, 1992).

[71] This particularly degrading kind of boundary violation is covered more fully later in this chapter.

> *would not capitulate to his demands that day, he chose to withhold being a father to the children, just to punish me.*
>
> *Two days later it was another special day, my youngest son's birthday. My husband did the same thing, withholding offering good from my son, because he did not get his expectations met with me. Again I refused to capitulate, but the sadness was felt by everyone. My son recalls that, as the most sad and disappointing birthday he ever had, because his dad never came out to celebrate it. This became a pattern for my husband to punish me with, for not giving him what he wanted when he wanted it.*

Indulging in pornography

The pornography that is so common among male abusers reveals their disdain for women and confirms them in their sense of superiority over their victims. Pornography portrays women in the most degrading manner, confirming in the abuser's mind his ideas about what women should be used for.

Also, because of the boredom of royalty, many abusers are constantly seeking some new form of stimulation. By lusting and getting orgasms from pornography, they obtain pleasure that temporarily quenches the thirst of their sin-sick souls.

"Stay in your marriage and try harder"

For almost two chapters we've talked about abusive tactics that avoid the obvious appearance of endangering the victim's life. For many Christian pastors, counselors, and church-goers, this means that the victim has no grounds for complaining about her marriage. After all, "we're all sinners," and "it takes two to cause marriage problems."[72]

Our Christian communities need to understand that though the following section describes cruelty at the highest levels on the scale of abuse, all the previous sections have described abuse that still needs to be addressed as abuse rather than simply "marriage difficulties."

---

[72] More about the poor counseling offered by church leaders is addressed in chapters 6 and 7.

Terrorizing the victim

Abusive people who claim to be Christians can be even more dangerous than many non-Christian abusers. These are the kinds of people Jesus referred to in Matthew 23:33 as a "brood of vipers."

Threats and cruelty

An abuser can exercise great cruelty against his victim without ever touching her and without even raising his voice. This can be, for example, through describing in detail the terrible things he will do to her or those she loves if she doesn't obey him.

> *The abuse started as soon as we were married. But for years I never dared to say anything to anyone about what was happening, because he said if I ever breathed a word—even to our pastor—he'd disappear, and I'd never see him again. So for a long time I just kept quiet. I wanted so much for our marriage to work out and become a beautiful thing that would bring honor and glory to the Lord, and he knew it and used that desire against me. He said that it was absolutely no one else's business what went on in the privacy of our home, and if I ever said a thing, even in confidence to ask for help, I would be a disobedient wife and in direct rebellion since he'd explicitly forbidden me.*
>
> *He was always adding more threats, too—he said that if I ever dared leave, he'd burn the house down with everything in it. He said he'd cut me off from all our accounts and make sure I was without a dime, and he'd take the children from me and ensure I'd never see them again. He also threatened to kill himself—and sometimes all of us, too—claiming I drove him to it, and once, on the way to church, when all of us were in the van, he purposely almost drove off a bridge on the interstate.*

He may also practice blackmail, such as threatening to post embarrassing or damaging material on the internet to compromise her, so that she won't report his illegal activities to the police. The abuser's threats don't have to be verbal; sometimes they can be communicated even by a look or a gesture that no one else but the victim will understand.[73] One abuser's relative said that he forced his wife to have a lesbian relationship with another woman for a period of time; then later he made explicit lesbian gestures to his wife in public, so that he could shame her, blackmail her, and control her.[74]

> *There was an unspoken language between us. I knew what he wanted, and I knew that if I didn't act accordingly, I and the children would be punished.*
>
> *He would put his arm around me in church, rubbing my shoulders, close to my neck. It looked like he was being sweet, but it was really a threat.*

The control of cruelty can also be accomplished through abuse of his victim's pets or other animals.

> *He broke the dog's legs for coming into the house muddy—after he let the dog out in the rain. Then he told me it was my fault because I insisted on the house being so clean.*

> *He was always cruel to the animals. He would beat them and throw things at them. He dragged calves around on the ground by chains tied around their necks and told us to look the other way if we didn't like it. He refused to give them adequate food or shelter, and a lot of them ended up dying from exposure in the harsh northern winters. The cows were emaciated and nearly died of starvation several times. The children and I always tried to feed them and protect them from the elements as best we could, but whenever he found out, he would rail against us for being rebellious and sitting in judgment on him for the way he chose to run his farm. When he stopped feeding the pigs grain, we started finding severed pig heads in the yard, because the sows were eating their piglets to try to get enough nourishment. When we tried to tell him, he accused us of turning against him and undermining his leadership of our family.*

---

[73] This is one reason couple's counseling is so counter-productive and even dangerous in an abusive marriage.

[74] In this case the relative didn't know if the abuser used his wife to produce pornography, but this is not unusual in abusive marriages. The threat of this pornography being made public can be a very effective means of blackmail.

Raging and physical violence

*The wicked watches for the righteous
and seeks to put him to death.*[75]

On our blog, www.cryingoutforjustice.com, many abuse victims have used the term "walking on eggshells" to describe the life they and their children have had to live with their abuser. They never know what might set him off and send him into a rage.

> *He would look for ways to destroy things that had value to me. I'd discovered a maple tree in the yard when it was just a sapling, and the children and I had nurtured it for nearly twenty years. Then one summer, with nonchalant, calculated malice, he went out and without preamble destroyed it with the chainsaw. One day in a violent rage he stormed into the house, and—while I was still in it, nursing the baby—he bludgeoned my recliner with a hammer over and over again until it was far beyond repair.*

Raging can be kindled in a microsecond and brought under control just as quickly, as the abuser pauses his tirade for a phone call or a knock at the door. He can rage by throwing or kicking things or smashing his fist into the wall. He can violently force open a locked door where his victim is hiding and brandish weapons. He may block her path and rip her clothes off in front of the children.

The abuser's lack of conscience, empathy, and appropriate shame permits him to rampage until, after his rage is spent, everyone in the household has become a quivering mass. Even when he appears to be out of control in anger, though, he is careful not to damage anything he values. His rage is actually more an intentional act of evil than a "loss" of temper or control.

> *In February, my "Christian" husband went from calm to raging in literally two seconds.... He smashed a TV tray into a million pieces when he slammed it into the love seat, then he picked up his practice club (like a golf club but weighted, so it's heavier) and proceeded to beat the floors and*

---

[75] Psalm 37:32.

> *other things with it. He started to swing at the TV, but decided not to. I picked up the phone, not knowing who I was going call. He saw me and dared me to call the police, because he was ready to bash their "f---ing skulls in" with his club. He gouged out big chunks of the linoleum at the back door, even chipped the cement underneath from pummeling it with his practice club. He took a bag of fast food we had just bought and threw it up the stairs. There was food everywhere. Condiments splattered all over the walls and ceiling. Grease spots on walls and carpet.*
>
> *What was he screaming about? His elderly mother and how he wanted to kill her; my dad, and how he wanted to kill him; how he wanted a family and I was denying him children because he's "not worthy" and he "doesn't behave" and he's "not nice" (all his words); how I cared about everyone else more than I did him. Then he called me a "f---ing c-nt."*

All of this, and he still hasn't "touched" her. What would your church do?

When the abuser becomes physically violent against his victim, he can carefully hurt her in places where it won't be seen. Her sleeves can cover those fingertip bruises on her arms—maybe no one will question why she's wearing long sleeves in the summertime. Or he can command her to wear her hair to cover the bruise. Most likely everyone will believe that she's extremely clumsy and runs into doors all the time.

What would many church members do if one of their own were arrested for injuring or even killing his victim? Perhaps, they may theorize, the pressures in his life meant that he wasn't himself. But when an abuser appears to be "not himself" to those of us on the outside who see the respectable Dr. Jekyll, maybe he is really being true to the Mr. Hyde character that he really is.[76]

> *I remember my abuser [a "good church man"] coming home from work in a rage. In fear, I ran to my son and locked us in his room. I put my weight against the door as he pounded on it. I begged him to stop as my son cried. Eventually the door flung open and I became pinned against the wall.*
>
> *The nightmare didn't end there. I grabbed my young son and made it to our SUV. I frantically buckled him into his car seat, while fumbling over a*

---

[76] Bancroft, *Why Does He Do That?* pp 34-36.

> *now very bruised and sore arm. Just as I jumped into the driver's seat, the door to the garage flung open. I looked on in horror at the realization that he had a large butcher knife in his hand. I desperately tried to start the car when I heard the back hatch open. He crawled up to the back seat and I prayed the rear view mirror was lying as I saw the blade approach my son's neck.*
>
> *I pleaded with him to just let us go as I grabbed my cell phone and dialed 911. I prayed that he wouldn't hurt my son for doing so, and finally felt a small sense of relief when the dispatcher answered the phone.*
>
> *When he heard the dispatcher on the phone he backed away. I drove off, but could only make it one street over as I was too shaken to drive. The police met me and arrested him when they saw the bruises on my arm.*
>
> *I wish I had left then, but I called my mom and she actually yelled at me for calling the police. "Calling the police on your husband is just not something you do!" Those words forced me to face so much more than I should have.*

Becoming the hero

Even in the middle of periods of terrible abuse, though, an abuser will look for opportunities to be the "hero" for his victim. Often it comes in the form of "saving" her from other people in her life who "just want to use her," possibly people who are learning that there is abuse in the relationship. He will fabricate the emergency, and then he will rescue her from the emergency, her hero.[77] The very man who perpetrates the terrible, mind-twisting abuse against the victim is the same one who comes to her rescue as her hero from the "unsafe" outside world.

> *Once my grandparents found out what Dad was like at home, they did all they could to be there for us. They called every week to see how we were doing and came often to visit. But we were afraid of them. Dad was always giving us elaborate interpretations of their behavior to "help us" see how "dangerous and devious" they were. Grammie and Grampie didn't really care about us, he said. They were just trying to stick their noses into our personal business because they wanted to break up our family. They wanted to have the state take us children away and send us to be*

---

[77] Ibid., pp 220-222.

> *indoctrinated in the vile, depraved public schools. They were always trying to undermine his authority, he said—the treats they brought were full of poisons like trans fats and soy, and the clothes they gave us had far too much "outward adornment" like bright colors and bits of lace. He would inspect everything they brought and send it back home with them if it didn't pass his approval.*
>
> *He said that they hated him, but that was okay—he was glad to be the "bad guy" to protect his family and keep us from violating our consciences.*

Master of the bedroom

> *They say that marital rape is whenever sex happens that the woman doesn't want, but they never talk about how abusers will argue that "not wanting it" is a sin before God. In the circles we were in, wives were carefully schooled on how Scripture teaches that "the wife hath not power of her own body, but the husband." There was no balancing, no calling the husbands to "live with their wives in an understanding way" including the way in which they demanded sex. The wife's needs weren't part of their equation at all. In fact, were she to try to make her needs part of the equation, she was robbing her husband of his due and would be responsible for tempting him to wander.*

The abuser will violate his victim's sleep boundaries by awakening her in the middle of the night to verbally attack her or to demand sex. But one of the most heinous ways an abuser violates appropriate boundaries is one that many Christians feel too squeamish to talk about.

What would you say if a woman told you that her husband rapes her? But sex is the most intimate of human relationships; it only stands to reason that it would be one of the abuser's favorite tools to establish supremacy over his victim. As perverted by the abuser, sex becomes one of the most cruel and destructive weapons in his arsenal.

In an abusive marriage, sex is used as a weapon of domination and control. Using the excuse that "marriage is honorable in all, and the bed undefiled,"[78] "Christian" abusers justify themselves in purposely

---

[78] Hebrews 13:4, King James Version.

inflicting pain on the victim during sex, using the victim for pornography, and raping them anally and/or with instruments.

How many women in our churches have been raped the week before by the very person sitting next to them?

Sexual abuse of children

If people with no conscience, no empathy, and a sense of entitlement view their children as objects for their service and pleasure, then it follows that many of them would be prone to sexually abuse their own children. About half of the women I've spoken with have told me that their abuser also sexually abused their children, creating an extra dimension to the dynamic of toxic shame in domestic abuse victims. [79] Dale Ingraham, a pastor who married the daughter of an abuser, tells their story in memoir form throughout his book *Tear Down This Wall of Silence: Dealing with Sexual Abuse in Our Churches (an introduction for those who will hear)*.

> *Faith's growing-up years were a nightmare. Behind the four walls of their house, their [pastor] father would scream and yell, physically abusing her brothers and emotionally abusing her mother. He created chaos and fear in the home, often threatening suicide, in order to beat the family into submission. For Faith, when her dad began raping and molesting her, she felt as if she had nowhere to turn.[80]*

Abusers who don't commit blatant sexual abuse against their children may still violate their sexual boundaries through such activity as refusing to allow locks on doors, walking into the bathroom when the daughter is showering, making fun of a child's developing body, speaking or acting in a sexual way toward the mother while the children are watching, or refusing to practice modesty in front of the children. All of these can be considered sexual violations.

---

[79] Toxic shame is discussed further in Chapter 5.

[80] Dale Ingraham with Rebecca Davis, *Tear Down this Wall of Silence: Dealing with Sexual Abuse in Our Churches (an introduction for those who will hear)* (Ambassador International, 2015), p 57. This book explores in detail the effects of sexual abuse on victims, including shame, confusion and fear, shattering of love and trust, traumatic disorders, and struggles with faith.

Tattering of the soul

The next chapter will explore more closely the effects of domestic abuse on the victims. We close this chapter with these words from a victim of domestic abuse.

The days are dark; the nights ever darker.
The things he says, are they true? Oh how I wish I knew!
Nothing I do is right. He controls everything in sight.
Money – it is all his. Groceries – "Why did you buy this?"

Don't question anything he does. He says I'm unfit to raise my kids.
He says my children's lives I've ruined. Is it true? How could I do that?
Perhaps he's right. What does he see? Is there really all that bad in me?
He must be right; he knows me best.

What did I do, what did I say? Why does he tear me down this way?
Why don't I leave? The things he does no one would believe.
My mother's chair he chopped and burned.
My neighbor's cat he stalked and killed.

What's wrong with me? It must be me! To others he's so great!
He's kind and giving and makes a clean living
He is generous beyond belief. His friends all bow at his feet.
In front of others he is so kind.

It must be me. I'm out of my mind. It has to be me!
When did it start? I gave him my heart.
Our love seemed so great From the very first date!

But it happened so slowly; he took control of me
Just little things at first
Step by step until he had complete control of everything that was me!
My heart, my very soul came under his control.

Where do I turn, which way can I go?
I hurt so deeply but no one knows
His words cut deep to my core.
Away from him I'd like to soar.
No, I must keep going. Without him I can't survive.
On my own I'd surely die.

But how can I stay? It gets worse every day!
I have no bruises anyone can see. Oh how I wish he would slap me.
Then I'd leave, I know I would, but where would I go? I do not know.
Oh, help my tattered soul! [81]

---

[81] Written by an abuse victim, this poem is read every year at the Overcoming Powerlessness luncheon in York, Pennsylvania. Thank you to Fred and Bonnie Wilt and the Overcoming Powerlessness team for granting permission to use it.

CHAPTER 5

Aftershock: The Effects of Domestic Abuse

When the righteous triumph, there is great glory,
but when the wicked rise, people hide themselves.[82]

> *For at least a year after I escaped my adulterous abuser, I wore the colors of a bruise. Blue, gray, brown, black. . . . I'm still struggling to get out of the habit of dressing in dark colors, even though my life is much better. It takes a while for the heart to catch up with the head.*

Effects on the victim's view of self and others

Anxiety and fear

"Both depression and anxiety disorders are common among women whose primary love relationship is abusive."[83] And it only makes sense. Female victims typically say, "I live in fear."[84] They live in fear of what he'll do if he learns she spent money, fear of what he will say if she visits a friend, fear that she won't be able to remember all the new rules he's made, fear of losing friends if they find out about the abuse she lives

---

[82] Proverbs 28:12.

[83] Susan Brewster, MSSW, *Helping Her Get Free: A Guide for Families and Friends of Abused Women* (Seal Press, 2006), p 220.

[84] In my experience, male victims more often say "she is crazy" or "she is controlling." Less often do they say that they live in fear.

with on a daily basis, fear that he will kill the family dog, fear of what he might do to one of the children, fear that he will alienate or take her children from her, fear of what he'll do if he finds out she's thinking of leaving, fear that he will kill her, fear that God will kill her if she leaves him.

> *You can't hide anything, because God knows, and he has become god. I felt like I had to confess everything to him—confess, or pay the price.*

Many victims don't have a reprieve from this fear even when they're asleep. They live in fear of the trauma-induced nightmares. They sleep with fear that abuse will be initiated suddenly in the middle of the night.

The victim will also live in fear of what effects the abuse will have on her children. He manipulates their perspective as well as hers, he torments them, he may even threaten to kill them. Ultimately it may be the abuser's attacks upon the children that compel a victim to leave. And yet . . .

> *I am so, so, so, so scared to file [for divorce]. Everywhere I turn, men are treating their ex-wives horribly in the divorce process. One woman I know in town has been forced to turn over her four kids every two days and she now has to pay HIM child support.*
>
> *I am scared I won't be able to find a job and have to live on the streets or in our van. I can't move in with my elderly parents. And it wouldn't work to stay with a sibling as they all have big families and no room for us.*
>
> *My lawyer had mentioned that I could move back to my home state and work/live and then file for divorce there after six months. I am worried that would backfire. My husband is so sneaky and underhanded about the finances, I am worried he would totally ruin everything. Not to mention, what if he moved up there with us? I just don't know how to go about it.*

The abuser's children suffer in a similar atmosphere of fear. Much of their time is necessarily spent in doing their best to calculate how to simply stay out of the abuser's way so as to not set him off, or to try to second guess what he is expecting from them today.

> *Some times at church or at family gatherings I could tell she wanted the "I'm a good mom" praise from all of us. I'm not sure how I knew it, but I knew if I didn't come up and give her a hug and say "I love you" I would be in serious trouble at home for embarrassing her. Some days I was too angry, and I wanted people to know she wasn't a good mom. I would be resistant to her hug or other nonverbals and wouldn't say "I love you," even when she said it to me. Those were small rebellions I paid dearly for.*

Fear is used by tyrants to subdue even entire populations. All thoughts are focused on the abuser. Children of an abuser effectively grow up in an environment of slavery.

Disorientation and confusion

An abuse victim can feel like a person who is lost and disoriented in the woods. Through the abuser's denial and accusations and constant questioning and challenging of her motives and twisting of history, she comes to distrust her own perceptions of reality. The confidence she once enjoyed in making decisions diminishes.

His gaslighting tactics take their toll. She didn't really tell him it would be fine for him to be late to work, did she? She didn't really accuse him of not loving the children, did she? He says she's crazy for thinking it's any other way. Maybe she really is. . . .

> *My abuser exploited my anxiety about my weaknesses and insecurities That is, if life dealt me challenges, he tied that to the concerns I had about my weaknesses. He would blame me, then soothe me as I despaired. At first it was a subtle pointing out that I screwed it all up. Later it was forceful and name calling. In an intimate relationship, you share your deepest fears and concerns. With an abuser, they know how to exploit that for their own gain.*
>
> *I honestly felt that I created a messy life and he mopped up my messes and provided stability that I never seemed to have in my life without him. It did seem that when I left him (I did that a few times before getting free), my life unraveled. It took a long time to disconnect from the lie. To me it is a bizarre form of psychological enmeshment. It develops into a very distorted dependence between victim and batterer. I was dependent on him and he on me. Hard to comprehend if you haven't lived it.*

The victim becomes increasingly disoriented, constantly ruminating with self-doubt. She might even wonder if she is going insane.

> *He tortured me with emotional and psychological abuse until I thought I would lose my mind. During my time in that house of horrors, I contemplated suicide for the first time in my life. I can remember standing in the laundry room one day, feeling the terrifying experience of my sanity beginning to slip away.*

Children may also show signs of their own disorientation and confusion by wanting others to make simple decisions for them or by extending apologies that are far greater than the situation warrants. This kind of behavior can be a red flag to those outside the family, of the fear, disorientation, and confusion being experienced at home.

False guilt and toxic shame

When a person has done something against God or others that needs to be repented of and made right, then a sense of guilt is appropriate.

However, by all the tactics described in the previous chapters, abusers can convince their victims of guilt for things that they really didn't do. When a person feels guilty for something that he or she didn't really do wrong, this is false guilt.

> *I bought beautiful colors for my temporary home, and I wore pretty things, but that changed as my circumstances grew bleaker. I started dressing on the outside to match how I felt on the inside. I felt as if anyone looking at me could see how shamed and humiliated I was, as if I were wearing a red letter A on my chest. It didn't matter that the letter A belonged on him.*

The guilt you are feeling [for "causing" the abuse] is not true guilt. True guilt is brought on by a realistic understanding of your behavior and its consequences to yourself and others. False guilt is an oppressive burden that is not based on reality but on the warped views, ideas, and attitudes of others.[85]

False guilt cannot be relieved by confessing and repenting, if what is being confessed was not really wrong in the first place. The only way to be relieved of false guilt is to recognize that it is false and to understand the truth.

> *My most frequent thoughts as I struggle to escape my own fog are "What have I done wrong?" "How could I have done this differently (so he wouldn't abuse me)?" and, "Is it my fault?" This is the man I've loved my whole life, built my dreams and life around, and I struggle to let go of the person I thought he was. I'd rather believe it's me or something I've done wrong than give up the entire foundation of the life I've lived up to now.*
>
> *I hope someday to be in a place where I can honestly say with my head, heart and whole self . . . NOT MY FAULT!!! and have a happy, peaceful life that reflects that knowledge having been internalized completely.*

If the abuser can hold his victim in a sense of false guilt for more and more of her actions, thoughts, and attitudes, he will increase her sense of shame. As Steven Tracy says, "healthy shame is a gracious call to correction and cleansing so we can be what the Lord of the universe meant us to be. . . . It is a gracious call to repentance."[86] This is what the *abuser* should feel, but instead, through his verbal and emotional abuse, through his extreme and constant humiliation, he transfers the sense of shame to the victim.

But the shame the victim feels isn't about her conduct or situation, rather it is about her *value as a person*. She has the sense that she is worthless, filthy, trash, a mistake, unlovable, contemptible. This is *toxic shame,* and it deeply affects her sense of her own identity.

[T]oxic shame distorts our sense of dignity as divine image bearers and drives us away from God. Toxic shame distorts

---

[85] Dr. Gregory L. Jantz and Ann McMurray, *Healing the Scars of Emotional Abuse* (Revell, 2009), pp 35-36.

[86] Steven R. Tracy, *Mending the Soul: Understanding and Healing Abuse* (Zondervan, 2008), p 65.

reality by going beyond convicting us that we've *done* bad things that need to be forgiven. It whispers to us that we *are* bad and unforgivable. Instead of pointing out real sin we can address, toxic shame distorts our sin, our worth, and God's grace so that we can do nothing but hide in the shadows.[87]

As they grow up and have to deal with the memories of domestic abuse in the home, many children of abusers, especially boys, also take on themselves false guilt that the abuse was their fault or that somehow they could have and should have stopped it. The toxic shame they can feel as they loathe themselves for their inability to stand up to the abuser can create many other kinds of problems in their lives.

Loss of sense of identity

> When one of our daughters needed surgery in a large city, I was incredibly daunted by the prospect of having to navigate on my own. It wasn't even complicated—I had a place to stay the night before surgery, and all I had to do was call a cab to get to the hospital. After the surgery I would stay in the hospital with our daughter.
>
> I remember it seemed strange to me that I was so taken aback by this circumstance, because I knew it wasn't like me at all. As a young single woman I had been independent and adventuresome—driving across the country over 1,800 miles to graduate school and preparing to head overseas as a medical missionary. I'd even dreamed of skydiving.
>
> But for twenty years my husband had hammered into me how every man on the street was just waiting to take advantage of me and that any woman without a man at her side was surely asking for all manner of trouble. And although I willed myself to trust God to protect me that day, the years had taken their toll. I had become merely a shadow of my true self with an intimidation that no amount of logic could shake.

Many Christians believe that a Christian should never feel a sense of self-worth (appropriate self-esteem), thinking that this would be equated with pride. Rightly taught, though, the doctrine of self-worth is to be equated with the sense of the value of the individual that is the

---

[87] Ibid. Italics added.

very reason for our understanding that it is wrong to murder. Every person, no matter what they have done or believed, has intrinsic value and individual identity. This should be an obvious truth, but has been muddled by false teachings.

As Christians, we know that our greatest identity flows from who we are in Jesus Christ. He has told us that we are engraved on the palms of His hands.[88] In Christ we can more fully know who we really are and are called to be. In fact, it is in Christ that a person can really fully develop as an individual with an individual calling.

However, through manipulations of reality and weapons of degradation and terror, as well as through false teachings such as "submit without question" and "Christians are supposed to give up their rights," the abuser accomplishes a reverse metamorphosis in his victim, from butterfly to caterpillar.

> When one person seeks to be the sole source of feedback on the value, worth, strengths, weaknesses, personhood, and identity of the other, it can become quite destructive to that individual. Little by little the person you were has been chipped away, and the person that's left is not someone you like very much, but you are now too weak and worn out to resist. As a result, you are fragile and easily manipulated and controlled.

As the North Koreans seek to reduce the inmates of their concentration camps to see themselves as nothing more than animals or ID numbers, the victim of domestic abuse suffers from destruction of the human spirit. Ultimately she may begin to believe that her feelings, thoughts, and desires are of no value. Only *his* feelings, thoughts, and desires are worthwhile. She begins to feel like a non-person.

A woman described how she'd experienced years of verbal assaults, diminishment, and disparaging comments about her abilities, spontaneity, and positive approach to life's problems. Most were cloaked as "just a joke," a "helpful" criticism, or an "offhand remark" that she took "too seriously." Without her

---

[88] Isaiah 49:16.

realizing it, her basic nature was slowly eroding. After her marriage ended, she met an old college classmate who told her he remembered her as a confident, vibrant, and dynamic person. That was when she realized the degree to which she had lost herself, for she was no longer the confident person she'd been.[89]

As the abuser violates his victim's boundaries, tells her what she should and should not think or do, condemns her decisions, contradicts her perceptions, mocks and ridicules her achievements and interests, the victim progressively loses her likes and dislikes, as her dreams and hopes are effaced.

> *In my relationship with him, in some sick way I mattered, but I didn't matter. My performance mattered. My work mattered. My attitude mattered. But who I was did not matter. Only what I could give. Only what he could get.*

Like a land with no borders or boundaries, she progressively loses the sense that she has an individual identity, the expressions and extensions of her self.

> *I used to be a strong, outgoing person. Now a simple interaction at the grocery store leaves me replaying the moment over and over in my head. Was I rude, stupid, disrespectful? I am constantly questioning myself to the point that I have lost myself.*

Children of an abusive parent also suffer the erosion of a sense of personal worth. Because the abuser simply owns them as commodities, their development as individuals is stunted as they learn that they must focus all their efforts on pleasing him or else suffer the consequences. Just like the abuser's spouse, the children will suffer from inability to

---

[89] Patricia Evans, *Victory over Verbal Abuse: A Healing Guide to Renewing Your Spirit and Reclaiming Your Life* (Adams Media, 2011), Locations 187-203, Kindle edition.

make decisions or to establish likes and dislikes, because their sense of self is being swallowed up in conformity to the abuser.

> On the day he made a veiled threat, I knew the physical abuse would soon begin, and I made my escape. Only through God's grace and the counsel of my parents did I have the guts to leave, because I was so beaten down I felt completely worthless.[90]

Alienation from others

> And those who know your name put their trust in you,
> for you, O LORD, have not forsaken those who seek you.[91]

The dynamics of abuse alienate people from one another in many ways. Victims are quite typically estranged from their circle of relationships and often even from their own children and grandchildren.

Because the abuser mocks family members (especially his primary victim) and often encourages other family members to join in the mocking, the members of the family will often become alienated from each other. Because he may disclose personal, private information in embarrassing ways, they will be afraid to talk with each other. Because he will blame his primary victim for his own bad behavior, the resulting confusion and fear will further alienate them. The abuser may accuse the victim of being a negligent parent—and he may cause that accusation to be true, because people who live in a fog of confusion, fear, false guilt, toxic shame, and loss of a sense of individual identity will find it difficult to take care of their own basic needs, much less those of someone else.

> There were six of us in the family, but in reality we were all isolated by our abusive dad's total control. My two sisters and I all stayed in the same bedroom and all knew he could "visit" any one of us at any time. . . . We never really shared in each other's lives, or even thought about telling each other, because we knew if we did, he would make us very sorry. This was our "normal." We never knew it wasn't supposed to be that way.

---

[90] Comment on A Cry for Justice, www.cryingoutforjustice.com.
[91] Psalm 9:10.

After his rage or sexual abuse the night before, in the morning the abuser acts as if everything is fine and normal. In this way, he inculcates within the family members that they should never speak of the evildoing. Many abused spouses, though they may suspect sexual abuse of the children, don't investigate further to try to find out what else the abuser is doing. The dark secrets will be kept.[92]

The abuser has done his work well. He has created an environment in which each member of the family lives in a plastic bubble. They may fight and yell at each other, but they won't give away the secrets.

> I'm alienated. I don't have a family anymore. . . . It is almost like there is too much pain, almost like we push each other's buttons too much. That's how my family is now, we're divided. . . . I can get so-called love from my dad as long as I follow his rules and as long as I do the things my dad wants me to do and act the way he wants me to act.[93]

Effects on the victim's finances and health

The soul of the wicked desires evil;
his neighbor finds no mercy in his eyes.[94]

Poverty

One domestic abuse victim of our experience went from living in a high rise to sleeping under a bridge. But though most don't have stories that extreme, many domestic abuse victims do struggle financially, even living below the poverty level, because of their abuser's childishness or selfishness or laziness.

> When he showed me the piece of land he wanted to buy to build our house, I was hesitant. It was in the middle of nowhere, far from the nearest roads and without access to utilities. To win me over, he took me to tour

---

[92] *Tear Down This Wall of Silence* by Dale Ingraham explores the many far-ranging and long-reaching effects of sexual abuse. Alienation from others is only one of them.

[93] Ann W. Annis, Michelle, Loyd-Paige, Rodger R. Rice, *Set us Free: What the Church Needs to Know from Survivors of Abuse* (Calvin College Social Research Center and University Press of America, 2001), p 67.

[94] Proverbs 21:10.

another off-grid house. With their state of the art generator and battery-bank system setup, they were able to have all the normal modern conveniences—a hot water heater, washing machine, dryer, dishwasher, microwave, sewing machine—and he promised to do the same thing for me. In the end I came around, and we bought the property, agreeing that we wouldn't move there until there was running water and electricity.

But he kept pressuring to move, and in the end I gave in. We moved into a tent at first, and then lived in a series of campers and temporary shelters for the next eight years until he finally got the shell of the house framed. We immediately moved into it—the shack we were staying in had gotten far too small now that we had five children—and that's where we lived from then on.

He never did any work on it after that, and even though he made plenty of money as a research physicist, he never hired anyone to finish it either. Anything I tried to do myself to make it more livable, like frame some of the interior walls or put up temporary closets, only disgusted him. He never put in the windows—in 30-below-zero winters, all we ever had was a thin layer of plastic—and we never did get running water or electricity.

At the beginning we'd all talk excitedly about the things we'd do and have "once we got the electricity hooked up," but in later years he'd mock us and berate us whenever we dared to mention a dishwasher or clothes dryer. God had said that we were to work six days a week by the sweat of our brow, he said, and modern conveniences were merely evidence of trying to get out of the way God commanded us to live.

Symptoms of Post-Traumatic Stress Disorder (PTSD)

> I am weary with my moaning;
> every night I flood my bed with tears;
> I drench my couch with my weeping.[95]

Trauma is simply pain that is too overwhelming for a person to process. In *Trauma and Recovery*, Judith Herman states, "Traumatic events are extraordinary, not because they occur rarely, but rather because they overwhelm the ordinary human adaptations to life."[96]

---

[95] Psalm 6:6.
[96] Herman, *Trauma and Recovery*, p 35.

> *At the age of 63, after 40 years of marriage to my wife, my whole nervous system collapsed with sleeplessness, anxiety, fears, much confusion, financial concerns, and a growing isolation.*

Partly because of the faulty belief in many Christian circles that people are composed of two or three easily distinguishable separate parts (body and spirit or body, soul, and spirit) rather than a unified whole, many Christians have been taught implicitly or explicitly that PTSD is a non-issue. What happens to the body does not affect the soul or spirit, some teach, and the symptoms people experience come about because of their own sin rather than because of the effects of trauma.[97]

In contrast, the groundbreaking book *The Body Keeps the Score: Brain, Mind, and Body in the Healing of Trauma*[98] explores many scientific studies that have shown again and again that trauma—pain that a person is unable to process—is stored in the brain differently from other memories, and affects the whole person in a number of different ways. As a result of the trauma of abuse, domestic abuse victims often experience certain conditions or engage in certain behaviors. According to Bessel van der Kolk, who has studied trauma for over forty years, trauma has a profound effect on the most fundamental functions of the body. "Trauma reactions can result in a whole range of physical

---

[97] For example, in "Biblical Overcoming Anorexia and Bulimia," in *Crisis Counseling II* (Bob Jones University, Center for Distance Learning, 2011), Session 6 handout 1, we read, "Anorexia and bulimia . . . are sinful patterns of misdirected control which the counselee has developed in order to solve problems which have arisen in her life. Biblical counselors [should] approach these eating behaviors much as they would alcoholism, compulsive gambling, and homosexual lifestyles. They, too, are sinful patterns which require the following measures: 1) Restructuring of the counselee's life to avoid temptation and to break sinful habits; 2) Individual discipling toward a reconciled and growing relationship with Jesus Christ and to learn God's methods of problem solving; 3) Practicing new patterns of problem solving until they become habitual responses. Sinful habits are changed when the counselee repents of them, makes herself accountable for indulgence in her sinful behavior, and submits herself to godly counsel." One victim of domestic and sexual abuse, after receiving just such counsel for her anorexia, said that after repenting and repenting of her anorexia without any change, she was told that she must not have repented enough. The result was that she wanted to kill herself.

[98] Bessel van der Kolk, MD, *The Body Keeps the Score: Brain, Mind, and Body in the Healing of Trauma* (Viking, 2014).

symptoms, including fibromyalgia, chronic fatigue, and other autoimmune diseases."[99]

> *Interestingly enough, it is not uncommon for the abused to develop Post Traumatic Stress Disorder from prolonged and ongoing abuse. I did—I even spent a month in a trauma treatment center in the US during my three-year-long divorce process. Let me tell you, PTSD is physical. Abuse alters the brain chemistry and make up.[100] I had a brain scan while in treatment, and my amygdala was lit up like the 4th of July night sky. It not only reshapes the physiological and chemical processes of the brain, it literally reshapes brain matter.*
>
> *How is it then, that so many can deny the physical reality of the effects of abuse other than broken bones and bruises? Do we deny the presence of cancer in someone with cancer because it doesn't give them a black eye or broken rib? The physical consequences of emotional, financial, psychological and sexual abuse are very real, absolutely able to be medically documented (although very few women are ever in a situation in which this is possible) and directly related to the trauma of abuse.*

One victim who contacted us had been a competent business woman and a socialite before her abusive marriage. Now, although her abuser had been dead for several years, she still found the social interaction of going to the grocery store overwhelming. She had to spend hours preparing for the shopping trip, energy trying to interact with a few people while she filled her shopping cart, and hours recovering from the ordeal afterward.

> The scientific study of suffering inevitably raises questions of causation, and with these, issues of blame and responsibility. Historically, doctors have highlighted predisposing vulnerability factors for developing PTSD, at the expense of recognizing the reality of their patients' *experience*. . . . When the issue of *causation* becomes a legitimate area of investigation, one is

---

[99] Ibid., p 47.

[100] Carina Storrs, "Brain Scan Offers First Biological Test in Diagnosis of Post-Traumatic Stress Disorder," *Scientific American*, January 22, 2010. http://www.scientificamerican.com/article/ptsd-diagnosis-brain-imaging-meg-neural-communications/

> inevitably confronted with issues of *man's inhumanity to man,
> with carelessness and callousness, with abrogation of responsibility,
> with manipulation and with failures to protect.*[101]

The domestic abuse victim may develop mental difficulties that would be described as personality disorders or bipolar disorders. A victim may try to cope by emotional numbing or self-medicating through drugs or alcohol. She will most likely develop health problems, sometimes mysterious, usually serious. Of the victims who have contacted me over the years, I've seen that poor health is almost always a common denominator. Living with constant stress and fear, depression, lack of sleep, hopelessness, nightmares, and toxic shame, takes a significant toll on the victim's health.

> Study after study shows that stress is a destroyer of health, causing disease and disability. The emotional toll of abuse is manifested in physical stress. Anger, guilt, and fear produce specific physiological reactions that wear down the body. Over time this stress produces physical symptoms that are impossible to ignore or medicate. These can include: digestive difficulties including ulcers and irritable bowel syndrome, heartbeat irregularities, chronic fatigue, tightness of the chest, difficulty breathing or hyperventilation, muscle tension or shakiness, headaches, loss of appetite, binge eating, chronic illness such as colds or flu, yeast infections, panic attacks, jaw disorders such as night-grinding of teeth and temporomandibular joint syndrome (TMJ), high blood pressure.[102]

PTSD symptoms in children

Abuse has terrible effects on children as well, whether they experience it first-hand or only second-hand by watching it occur.

---

[101] Bessel van der Kolk, *Traumatic Stress: The Effects of Overwhelming Experience on Mind, Body, and Society* (The Guilford Press, 2006), p 6. Italics added.

[102] Jantz and McMurray, *Healing the Scars of Emotional Abuse*, pp 44-45.

> *And what of the physical consequences to the children who witness abuse? Raised cortisol levels due to prolonged exposure to trauma,*[103] *and abuse is absolutely traumatic in whatever form it takes, changes the physical makeup of children's brain tissue and how their brain develops.*

Any of the following behaviors in a child can signal to an outsider that there might be abuse in the home:

- Developing an elaborate fantasy world (to escape from the abuse).
- Developing skewed attitudes toward people of the same gender as their abused parent.
- Violence or bullying toward other children or rebellion against authority.
- Engaging in reckless, dangerous, and even deviant behavior such as stealing, pyromania, vandalism, sexual play, eating disorders, and torturing animals.
- Developing addictions to drugs or alcohol, violent video games, or sex.

Especially if a protective teenage son is goaded and threatened by his father, as was described in Chapter 4, he may sink into deep depression and suicidal thoughts. He may even decide to kill the abuser, thinking that he may be able to help his family members escape, even if he has to sacrifice himself.

> Because post-traumatic symptoms are so persistent and so wide-ranging, they may be mistaken for enduring characteristics of the victim's personality. This is a costly error, for the person with unrecognized post-traumatic stress disorder is condemned to a diminished life, tormented by memory and bounded by helplessness and fear.[104]

---

[103] van der Kolk, *The Body Keeps the Score*, p. 61.

[104] Herman, *Trauma and Recovery*, p 49.

Physical injuries from assault

> *Keep me as the apple of your eye;*
> *hide me in the shadow of your wings,*
> *from the wicked who do me violence,*
> *my deadly enemies who surround me.*[105]

When abuse continues to escalate, domestic abuse victims ultimately end up in the emergency room . . . or the morgue. This, finally, is the point at which many Christians would acknowledge that abuse has truly taken place.

Batterers break their victims' bones, rip out their hair, choke them, shake them, give them black eyes and mammoth bruises, knock out their teeth, and rupture their stomachs. But physical injuries can usually heal.

> I've just divorced after 35 years of living with a wolf in sheep's clothing. His facade of Mr. Nice Guy hid a malevolence directed solely toward me. The physical violence began when I was pregnant with our first child, strangulation, fractured ribs, strike to the head that made me see stars. . . . These all healed. His gaslighting, blame-shifting, cycle of abuse, emotional unavailability, inappropriate relations with other women, sexual addiction, pornography and the objectification that goes with it . . . it's the emotional scars that take time.

Effects on the victim's view of God

> *Whoever says to the wicked, "You are in the right,"*
> *will be cursed by peoples, abhorred by nations,*
> *but those who rebuke the wicked will have delight,*
> *and a good blessing will come upon them.*[106]

> I had stopped going to church, and the kids had both left the house. I was left alone with my wife. As time went on I became virtually paralyzed, afraid to do most things required to simply live. Nothing made sense. I even questioned God and myself—a lot.

---

[105] Psalm 17:8-9.
[106] Proverbs 24:24-25.

One of the most insidious effects of the "Christian" abuser is the assault on the victim's Christian faith. The abuser plays his charade at church so flawlessly; he may even be a church leader. For both the primary victim and the children, seeing this rank hypocrisy fills them with questions that attack the validity of the truth of who God is and what He is doing.

> We would have to go to church, and it didn't matter what was happening. It didn't matter how bad the chaos was, but we had to pack up and dress up and act like life was wonderful and go and sit in church, and it didn't make much sense to me.[107]

How can there be any truth to Christianity if this is what Christians do? How can Christians be so hypocritical?

> From my prayers and Bible reading, I know God does not wish to see one of his daughters in this terrible place and in this emotional pain and anguish . . . but it's not heart knowledge a hundred percent of the time either.

Even victims who truly want to know and love God can be so traumatized in their lives that they can't access the truth. It's as if the truths about God that the victims most need to hear—God is love, Jesus died for you, He is your Rescuer, He is your Good Shepherd—are filed away in a filing cabinet of the brain, but the trauma of the abuse is what the victims live out in full color, with all their senses on hyper-alert.

> How is God going to meet me in this? I feel so desperate and needy right now, and I just fail to see how God is going to provide.

Because they are told they're bad, the victims, both spouse and children may feel themselves vile, unlovable, unreachable, beneath the gaze of an angry God who is always shaking a finger and glowering at

---

[107] Ann W. Annis, Michelle Loyd-Paige, and Rodger R. Rice, *Set us Free: What the Church Needs Know from Survivors of Abuse* (Calvin College Social Research Center and University Press of America, 2001), p 24.

them with a look of disgust. They may repent again and again of the same perceived sins. They cannot see God as a loving and nurturing Father whose arms are open wide to joyfully receive and protect them as beloved children.

> *I know God's love for me, but I can't seem to feel it. All I feel is pain and fear. I long to experience His love and protection, but the very one that should be an example of Christ to me is the one hurting me. Where is God? Is this God? Why won't He protect me?*

So where is the best place for the abused spouse and abused children to go to find support and help in their efforts to escape the abuse and understand the truth about God?

The church, of course, isn't it?

Isn't it?

CHAPTER 6

The Church Has Enabled Abuse

Finally, brothers, rejoice.
Aim for restoration, comfort one another,
agree with one another, live in peace;
and the God of love and peace will be with you.[108]

The deadly combination of ignorance and arrogance

What usually happens when someone reports abuse?

A common scenario when a domestic abuse victim reports abuse to her pastor proceeds more or less this way:

He doesn't believe her story, or believes it is exaggerated. After all, he reasons, it takes two to make marriage problems, everyone bears some fault in every marriage, and of course she has issues as well.[109] He is also certain that the one she is accusing is a genuine if not model Christian. He tells her to try to improve as a spouse and parent. He tells her to trust

---

[108] II Corinthians 13:1. Notice that this verse assumes that both parties desire this restoration and peace. We might as well apply this verse to the devil as to apply it to an abuser who masquerades as a godly man in the church.

[109] Some church counselors have stated that the marriage partner coming for help is the one with the problem.

the Lord, prays with her, and sends her home to her abuser, believing he has done what he should do.[110]

The victim prays more, repents more, and tries harder, but the abuse doesn't stop. The pastor may then do some couples marriage counseling, but the abuse continues and escalates. The victim continues to ask for help, but since she is the one making the commotion, she is seen as the problem. She is told to stop rebelling, forgive, and submit. Sympathies turn toward the abuser, the one who has such an "unsubmissive" wife.

Church leaders ignore her cries, deny or minimize the abuse, refuse to report the abuse to law enforcement, and decline to practice appropriate church discipline on the abuser.

> *I had tried to reach out to my pastor a few times for help after abusive episodes. My pastor usually saw me as overly emotional. My husband was seen as an upstanding Christian—a very good man. People felt sorry for him for having such an unsubmissive wife.*
>
> *After years of counseling together, where he manipulated all the sessions and I was repeatedly told to submit, I went back to the pastor to call out my husband in his drug addiction.*
>
> *The pastor met with us—he refused to meet with me alone, as I was a woman. Once there, the pastor told my husband everything that I had confided in him. I could feel the tombstone being carved right then and there.*
>
> *The pastor asked him if he was using drugs. My husband denied it. The pastor asked him to empty his pockets. He did, and the pastor saw the evidence with his own eyes—a pocket full of pills, enough to last a month or more. In response, the pastor put it on me to help him and hold him accountable—while still being submissive. No further help or counsel was offered.*

If the victim leaves the abuser, often *she* will be brought into church discipline, while the abuser remains in good standing in the church. The

---

[110] As one victim said about her church counselor, "For him, this is just an hour out of his week. But for me, this is my destroyed life."

victim is shunned and often is ultimately excommunicated. She will lose longtime friends and even family members.

This is not a rare occurrence. A host of victims have testified to this same course of injustice.

> They took my counseling notes from the times I had spent in counseling with them, and ended up hanging them on the walls of their "church" for any and all to view. They passed them around on iPads, email, etc. and printed them out for those who asked to see them. These notes contained explicit details of the abuse I had suffered at the hands of my abuser, including sexual abuse. The wife of [an elder] wrote taunting and degrading commentaries and lies within the body of these notes, ridiculing me and making fun of me for desiring sexual purity in my marriage. . . . Their words [about the abuser] were, "he is a baptized member in good standing and therefore, a Christian". . . . [They] degraded me publicly and falsely accused me, giving me no opportunity to speak, except to answer their charges against me as "guilty" or "not guilty."

Making the matter worse

Why do churches pour salt into the wounds of those who are the most wounded?

First is the very real possibility that a given church is swarming with wolves in sheep's clothing. No Christians want to believe that this is true of their own church, but God has told us in His Word that there are many false prophets, and thus we should test the spirits.[111] He warns us that Satan can appear as an angel of light. The servants of Satan can appear as sons of righteousness.[112]

But even in cases when the people of the church know and love Christ and want to see people be set free from sin, we still see situations in which abusers are protected and abuse victims blamed. Why would they minimize the abuse and render injustice to abuse victims?

A common cause for a wrong response to abuse is ignorance of the nature and tactics of abuse. Few Christians understand the ugliness of real abuse or how abuse affects its victims. When church leaders fail to

---

[111] I John 4:1.
[112] II Corinthians 11:13-15.

understand a problem, they cannot deal with it properly. But despite this ignorance, Christians commonly express a confidence that they have the ability to pronounce God's word on the situation.

> *I had gone to the pastors and elders, asking for help. Throughout our marriage my husband had continually abused both me and our children. But instead of addressing that, they insisted I set aside the fact of his twenty-five years of abuse and participate in couple's counseling to "move on from where you are now" (as the counseling pastor put it).*
>
> *I tried to help them understand why that was an unfruitful and even dangerous path to pursue until my husband was willing to acknowledge what he had done. It would be akin to forcing a conscientious whistle-blower to continue working for a corrupt, unrepentant, vindictive boss. I knew all too well—I had tried the couple's-counseling route many times in the past. My husband would always manage to charm and manipulate the counselor, casting himself as an unfortunate victim of a "conniving woman" and denying any wrongdoing. In the end, he had always twisted the sessions themselves into weapons of further abuse.*
>
> *The church, however, dismissed my concerns without even trying to understand. Fortunately, with the help of my domestic violence counselor, I was able to find another church.*

John MacArthur, Jr. is an example of a well-respected pastor and teacher who appears to be ignorant of the mentality and tactics of abuse. He limits abuse to physical only, and counsels victims to remain with the abuser ". . . if you are not truly in any physical danger, but are merely a weary wife who is fed up with a cantankerous or disagreeable husband."[113] Either the husband is physically abusing, according to MacArthur, or he is simply disagreeable. By these words, MacArthur shows that he is woefully uninformed on the subject of abuse.

---

[113] John MacArthur, "Answering the Key Questions about the Family," Grace to You Website, http://www.gty.org/resources/positions/p00/answering-the-key-questions-about-the-family

Other well-known and highly respected pastors[114] have also made it clear that they believe a woman cannot escape from her abusive husband unless she is in actual danger of life-threatening physical assault. For the most part, abuse victims are being told that God requires them to stay with their abuser, and usually the term *abuser* is not even used. This bad and even dangerous counsel shows that these leaders have never studied the nature of abuse in any depth or had any real training in the field.[115]

And you are arrogant! Ought you not rather to mourn?
Let him who has done this be removed from among you.[116]

Denying and minimizing abuse

A desire to remain ignorant

> *I had gone to our pastor two years prior, asking for help in dealing with my abuser and was told he doesn't get involved in marital issues because he was seen as taking sides and the couple usually ended up leaving the church. He suggested counseling (we had been in counseling five times over the years), and said he would pray for us.*

Especially in "marriage issues," people don't like to take sides. God names horrendous sins in the Bible, and abuse is among them, perpetrated by those who disguise themselves as good religious leaders.[117] But when we realize that this situation is in our own churches, it can turn our comfortable world upside down. Either a seismic shift in our practical theology needs to take place, or we can arrogantly exercise willful blindness.

---

[114] R.C. Sproul, *Now That's a Good Question* (Tyndale House Publishers, 1996), pp 404-405. Sproul has helped me immensely in understanding biblical doctrine, but he forbids divorce for abuse, even though he acknowledges that abuse is a violation of the marriage vows. If his views have changed in recent years, he has not publicly stated so.

[115] Many would say that no training in the field is necessary, because the Scriptures provide all the information that we need. Chapter 10 addresses this issue.

[116] I Corinthians 5:2.

[117] This would include the Pharisees as well as the wolves in sheep's clothing Paul warned the Ephesians about, as well as other examples such as the warnings in II Timothy 3:6 and Jude 1:4.

When Christians are ignorant about abuse and its deceptions, yet are arrogant enough to believe they are equipped to counsel any situation without truly learning about it, this creates an environment that an abuser can very easily manipulate. Ignorant and arrogant church people—those who are supposed to seek justice for the oppressed—become the evil man's ally. His abuse is either minimized or denied altogether.

> *After twenty-three years of verbal and emotional abuse, with me trying everything the books and preachers and "counselors" said to do to get him to stop, I finally got desperate enough to go to a couple I respected at church. I had recorded [my abuser] screaming at us for a spot he found on the ceiling (that had been there for four years and he was just noticing it). They listened to the five-minute-long rant, while I was sitting on their couch crying, and when I turned it off, they said, "He is an unhappy man." Then they said, "You [as in me? both of us?] are destroying your children." Then, "When I see you raising your hands in church, you are being hypocrites."*
>
> *I felt like my heart had been literally stomped under a jackboot and I could not breathe. Then they prayed for me, that God would give me the strength to stay and pray and "see it through." They then sent me back home, worse off than when I came to them.*
>
> *But I will say, God used that to finally make me realize, "These people don't get it. I don't need their approval." But it was a very painful and long-time-coming lesson for me to stop relying on man.*

When Christ told us to be as innocent as doves and wise as serpents,[118] he was saying that even though we want to be innocent of evil, we dare not be naïve about it. And yet, that's exactly what many believers are. Especially people who grew up in safe families and safe churches and safe schools can be incredibly naïve as to the realities of the dark deeds of hypocrisy. If we are to be the hands and feet of Christ, this arrogant ignorance must come to an end.

---

[118] In Matthew 10:16 Jesus says, "Behold, I am sending you out as sheep in the midst of wolves, so be wise as serpents and innocent as doves."

> *My husband has abandoned us now twice, committed adultery, hidden online gambling and pornography, now assaulted me and threatened me, and there is deep concern of inappropriate interaction with the children. The church believes it's me driving him to these things and making things up . . . being "manipulative." He is now very empowered, and I feel very afraid. I am supposed to just "obey" or else I will be excommunicated.*

The woman who wrote this was in fact excommunicated shortly after writing it.

A desire to protect . . . the wrong people

Based on the old pioneer tactic of bringing the pioneer wagons into a circle to protect the women and children while the men fought off the attackers, the concept of "circling the wagons" now describes several people working together to protect anyone who is under perceived attack. For example, how was it possible for well-known but abusive ministry leaders like Doug Phillips of Vision Forum and Bill Gothard of the Advanced Training Institute to continue in ministry for so long?[119] Why did it take years for their actions to come to light? It appears that the wagons were circled to protect reputations.

Church leaders will often circle their wagons around the accused abuser, because as a male (and sometimes even a church leader), he is "one of them."

> *The father runs the family. That's what we heard in church. That's what was preached. That's what we were taught in school, the male's role. And in our family—my family—my father was and is extremely religious in terms of being involved with church and church activities and everything else. The men were dominant.*[120]

---

[119] For example, regarding Doug Phillips, see Jamie Dean, "Doug Phillips excommunicated by church he founded," World, November 18, 2014, accessed via http://www.worldmag.com/2014/11/doug_phillips_excommunicated_by_church_he_founded Regarding Bill Gothard, see Warren Cole Smith, "Bill Gothard resigns from ministry," World, March 7, 2014, http://www.worldmag.com/2014/03/bill_gothard_resigns_from_ministry

[120] Annis, et al, *Set Us Free*, p 17.

Church leaders will also want to do all they can to protect the reputation of the church as an organization from scandal. If a high-profile person in the church is accused of being abusive, this does not look good for the church, and as a result, image protection can become the church leaders' top priority. In the name of "protecting the cause of Christ," the true cause of Christ—holy justice and His zeal to fight for the helpless—is ignored.

Micah 6:8 calls out: "He has told you, O man, what is good; and what does the LORD require of you but to do justice, and to love kindness, and to walk humbly with your God?" Anyone familiar with the Bible will realize that many verses like this one cry out for God's justice, to set things right for the oppressed against the wicked.

Fear

Most church leaders are not very familiar with the legal system, but when abuse is reported, suddenly it becomes up close and personal. It is a fearful thing to consider that someone you thought you knew is actually a very different person from what you thought, and may now face a long prison sentence. It is also fearful to think that the church and church leaders will come under legal scrutiny.

> But on the day I spoke with him, my pastor suddenly expressed great concern about himself. . . . I was concerned that now the pastor might be trying to just save his own skin in the situation, and I really didn't understand why he was so concerned. . . . The entire episode took on the aspect of a charade at times—with the church leadership trying to save its own skin, while turning a blind eye to what was happening to my daughter and me. . . . The pastor was more concerned about his own appearance than the injustices done to a child and wife. In all of this, neglect of the church flock is also a concern now that the wolf has been embraced back into the fold, while two sheep (my child and I) have had to flee the masquerade ball.

Misunderstanding of key concepts

One of the tactics church leaders will use is to tell the victim, "Look, he repented. So now you need to forgive. Then you can be reconciled."

What do church leaders typically think these terms mean? What do they really mean? How will this change the way abusers and their victims are counseled?

What is true repentance?

Christians have no excuse for being deceived by false repentance, but it happens all the time. The solution for this common phenomenon is to truly understand what real repentance is.[121] Repentance is a gift from God[122] to confess guilt, acknowledging sin.

True repentance is *responsible*, meaning that the offender will willingly shoulder the responsibility for the sin without minimizing, without excuses, without blaming anyone else, and without expecting change from another person.

True repentance is *unconditional*, agreeing that the offender is deserving of just punishment for his wrongdoing without qualification.

True repentance is *empathetic*, at least beginning to feel the pain and grief caused by the sin, without focusing on the guilty person's own desire for forgiveness from the offended person.[123]

True repentance is *redirectional*, resulting in a change of direction of the person's life and behavior.

It is fairly easy to spot false repentance. It will include language that will minimize the offender's sin ("I didn't do it all the time"), make excuses ("The door was broken anyway"), blame others ("She knows how to push my buttons"), expect changes from others ("If she stops doing that, I won't get so mad"), minimize or ignore the punishment deserved ("I've been made new and my sins are separated as far as the

---

[121] Christians desperately need to come to a correct biblical theology of repentance, forgiveness, and reconciliation. Wrongly handled, these become some of the favorite topics of the abuser's distortion, permitting him to manipulate his victims with "biblical authority." I recommend Barbara Roberts' Checklist for Repentance, which you can access at http://notunderbondage.com/pages/barbara-roberts-checklist-for-evaluating-an-abusers-repentance. See also Dale Ingraham's *Tear Down This Wall of Silence*, pp 150-153.

[122] II Timothy 2:25.

[123] Steven Tracy cautions that offenders can be expert manipulators. Tracy maintains that it is generally inappropriate for the abuser to ask the victim for forgiveness. Such a request pressures the victim and puts her in an unfair and harmful position. See his book *Mending the Soul: Understanding and Healing Abuse* (Zondervan, 2005), especially chapter 10.

east is from the west"), ignore the pain and grief of others ("I was messing up my own life doing this"), and insist on quick forgiveness ("I've experienced God's forgiveness, so I know you'll forgive me too"). Tears are often on display, but tears are no sign of the validity of a person's repentance.

> With my soon-to-be-ex-husband getting baptized yesterday, it has thrown me for a loop. He is professing to be a believer, and it looks like he is taking steps to change. He posted a video of himself being baptized (I admit, we had storms yesterday, and I was waiting to hear if lightning struck the church). So many people are commenting on his "new changes" and his faith. I am really struggling. . . . Am I wrong to question his "belief"? His family is all rallying around him and not one person has reached out to me and expressed anger or sorrow for the years of infidelity, porn, and abuse.

What is true forgiveness?

One victim explained to me that her "godly" father had lived a double life of physical violence and sexual abuse in the home. When he tried to murder his family members, the church argued that he had just gone insane, insisting on quick forgiveness and reconciliation.

In Matthew 6:14-15, Jesus said, "For if you forgive others their trespasses, your heavenly Father will also forgive you, but if you do not forgive others their trespasses, neither will your Father forgive your trespasses." These are sobering words, but we should not try to make them mean more than what God means when He says them. The true and complete meaning of forgiveness is this:

Forgiveness is a decision made by the offended one not to demand payment of the personal debt that the offender owes him.

This implies that the one forgiving will not seek personal vengeance.[124] This is all that true forgiveness entails, and it may be a long time coming, as the one who has been victimized comes to terms with what has actually happened.

Christians have added more requirements to forgiveness than the Lord has made, meaning that, like the Pharisees, they put grievous burdens on men's backs.[125]

Christians have said *forgiveness must be unconditional and total, requiring nothing on the part of the offender.*

But the truth is true forgiveness is conditioned on confession and repentance, just as God's forgiveness of us is conditioned on confession and repentance, according to I John 1:9.

Christians have said *forgiveness means forgetting the offense.*

But the truth is if the victim truly does forget an offense each time it occurs, she can be revictimized again and again and again. This way of thinking can ensnare victims in decades of abuse.

The truth is repeating the same sin again and again evidences a lack of true repentance, meaning that it may be impossible to dismiss consequences, and very likely unwise. In Acts 26:19-20, Paul said that he preached to the Gentiles that they should perform "deeds in keeping with their repentance."

> *When my husband confessed to years of marital infidelity and porn, we entered a separation period and started counseling. After some time, I extended forgiveness to my husband (believe me, it was God's grace which enabled me to do so!) which he seemed genuinely surprised and pleased about. From then on, when our reconciliation attempt didn't seem to be going anywhere (he refused to continue counseling, blew off any accountability at church, didn't want to change his job, etc.), and I would*

---

[124] I specify *personal* vengeance because it is still proper for a victim to implore God to effect His holy vengeance upon an unrepentant abuser. This is demonstrated by the imprecatory psalms, such as Psalms 7, 35, 55, 58, 59, 69, 79, 109, and 137, in which the psalmist implored God to bring justice and righteous vengeance upon his enemies. The Apostle Paul also used imprecation in Galatians 1 when he expressed his desire that those who distort the gospel be "anathema," or cursed by God.

[125] Matthew 23:4.

> *bring up my frustrations with the process, he said that I just needed to "forgive and forget." He said that my continually bringing things up to him meant I hadn't forgiven him, and instead just wanted to punish him.*

Christians have said *forgiveness means you won't think about the offense and you won't talk about it to anyone.* When a victim doesn't respond well to immediate talk of forgiveness and reconciliation, then in the minds of many she becomes the wrongdoer by showing "bitterness."

But the truth is in order to process pain from abuse and recover from it, and ultimately to be able to fully release the debt, the abuse victim must feel free to remember, think, and talk about it.

The memories must be allowed, if necessary, to swell, surge, subside, resurge, and recalibrate with truth. This is an important way that our minds are able to make sense of traumatic events.

The victim should not have to feel guilty about processing the trauma by venting with safe people, and discussing it, not only to reach a point of being able to release the debt, but also in order to find a way to avoid such trauma in the future.

> Many victim/survivors I know have tried to follow that kind of recipe (distorted forgiveness). They end up living somewhat tight, self-constructed lives, stuffing their feelings, blocking their history, being Job's counselors to other survivors, and always in danger of being re-triggered into fear or anxiety by relatively insignificant events that remind their subconscious of the big trauma they've tried to suppress.[126]

Christians have said *forgiveness means that we will not pursue negative consequences against the offender.*

---

[126] Personal correspondence with Barbara Roberts, 2012.

But the truth is we have Biblical precedent for praying that God will strike the wicked and deliver the victims to safety.[127]

The truth is it is appropriate to pursue justice through the legal system, according to Romans 13. It is appropriate for a criminal to be sentenced for his crimes, for the marriage whose vows have been broken to be dissolved,[128] and for the wrongdoer to undergo church discipline and even excommunication.

In II Timothy 4:14-15, Paul said to Timothy, "Alexander the coppersmith did me great harm; the Lord will repay him according to his deeds. Beware of him yourself, for he strongly opposed our message."

In the true sense of the word, Paul had clearly forgiven: he was not seeking personal vengeance against his offender, but trusted the Lord to repay him according to his deeds.

However, Paul had obviously spent some time thinking about his experience with Alexander. He was certainly bringing it up again. He was talking to someone about it, and a case could be made that he was "using it against" Alexander. He is stating very clearly that his personal relationship with Alexander had been hindered, with no desire to re-establish a relationship with him, and he also urged Timothy to be cautious around him.

Paul offers an example of a Biblical attitude of forgiveness toward a dangerous offender.

When does reconciliation occur?

> *I know if I stood my ground and said I would not reconcile, they would think I was the problem, not him … the bitter wife who will not forgive. I just did not want to subject myself and my children to the abuse anymore.*

Christians have said *forgiveness is evidenced by reconciliation.*

---

[127] Revelation 6:9-10, for example, says, " . . . I saw under the altar the souls of those who had been slain for the word of God and for the witness they had borne. They cried out with a loud voice, 'O Sovereign Lord, holy and true, how long before you will judge and avenge our blood on those who dwell on the earth?'"

[128] See chapter 7 for more on this topic.

But the truth is forgiveness is simply the agreement to refrain from pursuing repayment of a debt. This was the case with Paul in his treatment of Alexander in II Timothy 4:14-15.

The truth is a reconciled relationship is a relationship of re-established trust. This will require time, since repentance must be proven over time to be authentic, through the repentant one bringing forth fruits "worthy of repentance."[129] Indeed, though one who has been wronged may be willing to release the debt, the relationship of trust may never be re-established.

> *My ex-husband is a reprobate. . . . He wasn't interested in Christianity until we'd been separated for four years; then he accepted my invitation to come to an evening church service where he responded to the altar call and said the sinner's prayer. For the next few months he showed quite marked signs of true conversion: he loved to read the Bible and go to church and be with other believers. . . .*
>
> *Although at first I hadn't wanted reconciliation, I began to want it after seeing these changes in him. So we reconciled, renewed our vows, and within twelve months he had shed all his Christian coloring and was assaulting me again. Mind you, in those twelve months he'd been very verbally and psychologically abusive, but I didn't recognize what was happening till he assaulted me again. Once during those twelve months he'd even heard God telling him very sternly and specifically, "Go and tell your wife you are sorry for treating her the way you've been treating her, and ask her how she would like to be treated." I nearly fell off my chair when came home from work that day and told me what God had said to him. But his brief flash of reform didn't last even twenty-four hours.*
>
> *He remains unrepentant to this day. He has lied; he's never apologized to me, and he has told others a pack of lies to cover up the real reasons why I separated from him, divorced him, and eventually pulled the plug on all visitation.*[130]

When Jesus said in Luke 6:27-28, "Love your enemies, do good to those who hate you, bless those who curse you, pray for those who

[129] Luke 6:45; Genesis 42-45.
[130] Jeff Crippen and Anna Wood, *A Cry for Justice: How the Evil of Domestic Abuse Hides in Your Church!* (Calvary Press, 2012), pp 31-32.

abuse you," He was saying that, for example, if you see your enemy on the side of the road beaten by robbers, like the Good Samaritan you will do your best to get him help. He was not talking about establishing a relationship of trust with that enemy.

With an abuser, doing good to him and loving him most often means the opposite—keeping him out of the home. If he hasn't truly changed, then trusting him and yielding to his evil control is neither good nor loving.

More bad counsel for the victim

Christians, the body of Christ, the church, should be the strongest advocates for the innocent and weak. Though we should give genuine help to abusers, of primary importance we must affirm that our fundamental duty is to help and protect the weak and suffering—the victims. Sadly, victims often hear many of the following unhelpful admonitions instead.

Called to suffering?

It is common for abuse victims who reach out for help from fellow Christians to hear something such as, "God has called you to suffering, and He'll give you grace for it. Be thankful that you have not yet 'resisted unto blood.'"[131]

> I told another woman of my husband's spinning the car around with me and our daughter in it, for my merely requesting that he write himself a note. The woman replied, "Oh, my husband's done that too." Yet another woman whom I told of my husband's words at home said, "Oh, he's just a bully. My husband threatened to destroy all of my photo albums, but you know what? That's just stuff. All I need is Jesus." I did not believe this counsel to be Biblical, because it dismisses God's justice and allows wrong behavior to have its way.

Romans 12:1-2 tells Christians that we are to be living sacrifices. This phrase, preached and taught out of context, can cause many

---

[131] This is a de-contextualized reference to Hebrews 12:4.

domestic abuse victims who love the Lord to think that they should continue to allow the abuse, considering themselves as sacrifices in a physical sense. But perhaps the best explanation for "living sacrifices" is found in Romans 6:13, which says, "Do not present your members to sin as instruments for unrighteousness, but present yourselves to God as those who have been brought from death to life, and your members to God as instruments for righteousness."

This clearly says that God does not want us to allow our bodies to be used for evil—our own or anyone else's. Instead, He wants our bodies to be used for righteousness.

Scriptures such as Romans 5:3-4a emphasize the importance of suffering well, trusting God in the midst of suffering. Many abuse victims have stayed in their place of suffering because they have been told that it honors God to do so, to continue to "suffer well," being told that it is part of their sanctification.

> *Psalm 91:14-15 says, "Because he holds fast to me in love, I will deliver him; I will protect him, because he knows my name. When he calls to me, I will answer him; I will be with him in trouble; I will rescue him and honor him." I cried out to God. I held fast. But I was still alone and hurt. He uses Christians to be His hands and feet, but Christians are the ones condemning me to this fate, to remain in this nightmare of a marriage.*

A willingness to suffer well is commendable. But is all suffering to be endured indefinitely for the glory of God and His Kingdom? David hid from King Saul in the caves.[132] Does this mean he didn't suffer well? In the New Testament, Saul (Paul) escaped from the Jews in a basket over the wall of Damascus by night.[133] Does this mean he didn't suffer well? When a victim removes herself and her children from a place of abuse, this does not mean that she hasn't suffered well.

---

[132] I Samuel 21-31.
[133] Acts 9:23-25.

Considering the suffering that the abused is dealing with, it is appropriate for her to remove herself from the suffering and danger that the abuser is causing.

Don't gossip about your abuser?

During a testimony time in church, one victim spoke her thanksgiving to God that He had kept her safe through her escape from her abuser. Later the church leaders told her that speaking about her husband that way was inappropriate gossip.

Gossip: "idle talk, news mongering, tattling, spreading groundless rumors." But when our purpose is to share important information, and our motives are not malicious, talking with others is not gossip. In *The Socially Skilled Child Molester,* author Carla van Dam emphasizes that the insistence that we refrain from gossip helps to keep the abuser's cloak of secrecy in place.[134]

> For years I was told "you'll destroy him; who have you told; it's a private matter; here's what you need to do, etc." while I suffered. He cheated on me for at least three years . . . lied about it while we taught Sunday school, treated me horribly, but I am the outsider because I finally started talking to get help. I went three times to the pastors for help and support, with a binder full of proof detailing the lies, manipulation, and abuse. I got very little help; he was not held accountable at all and still attends and acts like nothing ever happened. The church even allowed him to attend a singles small group when he was still in our home. I've had to leave my church of twenty years.[135]

Another woman divorced her abuser, a well-known and well-respected Christian leader who had tried to kill her three times. When the divorce was final, her own church declared that it was wrong for her to ever reveal these "details."[136]

---

[134] Carla Van Dam, *The Socially Skilled Child Molester: Differentiating the Guilty from the Falsely Accused* (Routledge, 2006), p 92.

[135] Comment on A Cry for Justice, www.cryingoutforjustice.com.

[136] Catherine Clark Kroeger and Nancy Nason-Clark, *No Place for Abuse: Biblical and Practical Resources to Counteract Domestic Violence* (IVP Books, 2010), pp 118-119.

God does not want us to keep evil in the church a secret. His Word plainly teaches us that we should call out the evildoers publicly, in order for people to be warned and kept safe, and for them to be held responsible for their evil deeds.[137] Christians should be taught that neither sexual abuse nor domestic abuse should be hidden to protect the abuser. God names names.

We are all sinners?

Matthew 7:1 says, "Judge not, that you be not judged." People use this Scripture when they don't want to say or hear anything bad about the accused. But all of us make judgments about others at times. So how should this Scripture really be used? Matthew 7 indicates that we should confess our own sins and repent of them before pointing out the sins of others. This doesn't mean that we shouldn't judge at all—in fact, in other places, we are commanded to. For example, "Do not judge by appearances, but judge with right judgment."[138] "The mouth of the righteous utters wisdom, and his tongue speaks justice [judgment]."[139]

Many Christians fail to understand the truth that "Sin is always progressive; if it isn't confessed and repented of, it will grow worse and worse, to the point where it will destroy a person or a church or even a society."[140] Christians make a mistake thinking that all sin is the same, all sinners are the same, and the steps of counseling for all of them should be the same. This leads to enabling the abuser to further victimize his victims.

Matthew 18?

When I hear people saying "it's a church matter," most often they are referring to the Matthew 18 process of church discipline. This passage of Scripture advocates that issues between Christians should first be dealt with in private; if the private confrontation doesn't bring repentance, to

---

[137]For example, in I Timothy 1:20 Paul wrote, "among whom are Hymenaeus and Alexander, whom I have handed over to Satan that they may learn not to blaspheme." Also see I Corinthians 5; II Timothy 4:14-15; Galatians 2:11ff; III John 1:9ff.

[138]John 7:24.

[139]Psalm 37:30.

[140]Ingraham, *Tear Down This Wall of Silence*, p 13.

then go with two or three, and if that doesn't bring repentance, to take it before the church.[141]

However, Matthew 18 isn't a universal dictum. It applies to disputes, but not to abusive activity. We can say this because as far as we know, Jesus didn't go to the Pharisees in private before calling them out in public, in shockingly scathing terms. It appears that this is because their secret actions were of a criminal nature, the kind that need to be dealt with in a public way, for the purifying of the church and for the safety of society. Neither did Paul follow Matthew 18 in dealing with the scandalous sin at Corinth in I Corinthians 5.

Submit harder?

> Someone in the men's group told him he should humiliate me and make me an example to the other women in the church.

In *Lies Women Believe and the Truth That Sets Them Free,* Nancy Leigh DeMoss writes, "When we place ourselves *under the spiritual covering* of the authorities God has placed in our lives, God protects us. On the other hand, when we insist on having it our way and stepping out from *under that covering and protection,* we open ourselves up to the influence and attack of the Enemy."[142] And, "Our willingness to place ourselves *under* God-ordained authority is the greatest evidence of how big we believe God really is."[143]

What DeMoss is teaching here is not to be found in Scripture, but is instead what some have called Gothardism, the teachings of Bill Gothard, founder of the Institute of Basic Life Principles.[144] Gothard teaches that if a person gets out from under what he calls the "umbrella

---

[141] The people I've heard claim Matthew 18 largely don't follow through with church discipline and end up protecting the abuser.

[142] Nancy Leigh Demoss, *Lies Women Believe and the Truth That Sets Them Free* (Moody Press, 2001), p 148. Italics added.

[143] Ibid., p 149. Italics added.

[144] See, for example, Wade Burleson, "Bill Gothard: His Umbrella of Protection Teaching Provides an Umbrage for Perverted Behavior," http://www.wadeburleson.org/2014/03/bill-gothard-his-umbrella-of-protection.html

of authority," he or she will be in rebellion and will be susceptible to the attacks of Satan.[145] Teachings like this, which strike fear into the heart of an obedient Christian, can work to keep a victim in a domestically abusive situation far past the time when the situation has become intolerable for her and her children.

> *We listen to this false teaching because it is easier to believe, based on what we have been shown by our abuser, that we deserve punishment rather than grace. As women we are unworthy. As women we must submit.*

We must carefully explore what Ephesians 5:22-24 really means when it says, "Wives, submit to your own husbands, as to the Lord. For the husband is the head of the wife even as Christ is the head of the church, his body, and is himself its Savior. Now as the church submits to Christ, so also wives should submit in everything to their husbands."

Steven Tracy, author of *Mending the Soul: Understanding and Healing Abuse*,[146] has addressed the concept of submission in an article[147] that surveys a number of Christian books on the subject. In it he explains the concept of submission as "voluntarily yielding to another in love,"[148] rather than blind obedience. He notes that because husbands are not Christ, they cannot be obeyed without qualification. Regarding the phrase "submit in everything," he writes,

> But the New Testament makes it clear that allegiance and obedience to Christ trumps all other allegiances. Believers are never to obey a human authority who commands them to disobey Christ. So unless Paul is patently contradicting other Scriptural teaching, Ephesians 5:24 cannot mean that wives

---

[145] "What is an 'umbrella of protection'?" http://iblp.org/questions/what-umbrella-protection The website www.recoveringgrace.org, established in 2011, works to expose the teachings of Bill Gothard by which he bought others under his abusive leadership.

[146] Zondervan, 2008.

[147] Steven R. Tracy, "What does 'Submit in Everything' Really Mean? The Nature and Scope of Marital Submission," *Trinity Journal*, 2008, 285-312.

[148] Ibid. He goes on to explain that the military model of submission used by many Christians does not suffice as an explanation of the submission God requires between His people.

should submit to every single command or request from their husbands. . . . Paul commands wives not to obey every single dictate from their husband but rather to be broadly responsive to their husband's leadership instead of limiting their response to a few narrow issues of their choosing.[149]

In the spirit of Biblical submission, "voluntarily yielding in love," Tracy offers and supports six circumstances under which a wife should not obey her husband:

1. When obedience to him would violate a Biblical principle.

2. When obedience to him would compromise her relationship with Christ.

3. When obedience to him would violate her conscience.

4. When obedience to him would compromise the care, nurture, and protection of her children.

5. When obedience to him would enable (facilitate) her husband's sin.

6. When obedience to him would subject her to physical, sexual, or emotional abuse. [150]

Peter and the apostles said, "We must obey God rather than man."[151] This is true for abuse victims in a domestic setting as well as anywhere else. Only God has absolute authority. A man who justifies his abuse by citing "headship" is a tyrant and an enemy of God.

Win him without a word?

1 Peter 3:1-2 says, "Likewise, wives, be subject to your own husbands, so that even if some do not obey the word, they may be won without a word by the conduct of their wives, when they see your respectful and pure conduct." Based on this Scripture, abuse victims have been told that if they will persevere in their marriage no matter the cost, God will win the husband over. However, I Peter 3 refers to clearly

---

[149] Ibid.

[150] Ibid.

[151] Acts 5:29.

unsaved husbands rather than abusers who wear a mask of deception by claiming to be Christians.

Nancy Leigh DeMoss references this Scripture to say, "A wife's submission to her husband, regardless of his spiritual condition, actually releases her from fear because she has entrusted herself to God, who has ultimate control of her husband and her situation."[152] DeMoss makes it clear that she has no understanding at all about abuse, because some women who are trying to practice unqualified submission live in constant fear.

> It was not only the church leaders who surprised me by their reaction to the problems in my marriage and ultimate divorce, but even more the women of the church. I noticed throughout the eight years I was at that church that whenever I'd speak of behaviors that my husband would exhibit at home, nearly every woman in whom I confided ultimately encouraged me to greater silence, placating, forgiving, and submitting.
>
> In one women's study group when I spoke of my husband's passive-aggressive [i.e., covert aggressive] behaviors, a lady wrote out Psalm 141:3 on a scrap of paper and handed it to me. It read: "Set a guard over my mouth, Lord. Keep watch over the door of my lips." As she handed it to me she stated that my husband doesn't want to hear about God or anything else I have to say. She said he already knows and that my talk at home was likely an annoyance.

In the book *Me? Obey Him?* Elizabeth Rice Handford admonishes women, "God has made a promise to the woman who will obey her husband. He keeps His promises. He will not honor disobedience, no matter what excuse is given for it. A woman wins her husband, draws him to a higher spiritual plane, by a submissive, quiet spirit. . . . Yes, it really works. God will bless your home if you are obedient."[153]

---

[152] DeMoss, *Lies Women Believe*, p 150.
[153] Elizabeth Rice Handford, *Me? Obey Him? The Obedient Wife and God's Way of Happiness and Blessing in the Home* (Sword of the Lord Publications, 1995), p 77. One woman in an abusive home bought copies of this book and gave them away, believing that as she waited and submitted, God would rescue her marriage. After many years, she and her children finally escaped from their abuser.

In endorsing the wife's blind obedience and claiming without reservation that this will bring her husband into submission to Christ, Handford ignores the obvious disobedience of the abuser. "[God] will not honor disobedience," she says, "no matter what excuse is given for it."[154] Indeed. When a husband is living in disobedience to God, it is appropriate for his wife to choose to "obey God rather than man."[155]

As she refuses to obey a husband who is walking in disobedience, the wife is taking action that God will honor.

Keep no record of wrongs?

First Corinthians 13:5 has caused trouble for abuse victims who are trying to document their abuses so that someone will believe them. The New International Version of the Bible says love "keeps no record of wrongs." The King James Version says love "thinketh no evil." The English Standard Version says love is not "resentful."

It happened multiple times. When I would go to the pastor for help with our marriage, he would press me for specific examples of what I was talking about. This was always tricky, because I worked really hard to never keep lists, even mentally. I wanted issues to be addressed, but I didn't want to hold grudges, and it was easier to keep from being bitter if I was truly not holding onto the specific things he had done.

But when I tried to explain this to the pastor, he said he really needed more particulars if he was going to be able to get anywhere. He directed me to keep a record detailing the issues that arose between now and the next time we met. So I did.

But when I brought out the list at the next session, the pastor castigated me severely. I was a bad wife, he declared. Love was to keep no record of wrongs but was to forgive and forget. I needed to search my own heart and repent of my bitterness. And just like that, the rest of our meeting was spent detailing my supposed failings as a wife. All because of a list I'd made only because he'd required it of me.

---

[154] Ibid.
[155] Acts 5:29.

In *The Emotionally Destructive Marriage*, Leslie Vernick addresses the sense of guilt that I Corinthians 13:5 can cause in women who are trying to document their husband's behavior.

> This verse doesn't tell you to forget about what happens. That could be very dangerous. This verse tells you not to keep score. Not to allow your anger and hurt to harden your heart with resentment and bitterness that make you feel entitled to retaliate.[156]

You are codependent?

In my line of work, I receive many letters. One abuse victim had written a description of a typical day in her life for her counselor, trying to show how the abuse had increased over the course of the years of her marriage. This woman told me that through the years she had asked the Lord to show her her own sin, wanting to change herself, especially because her husband would not change. When she read her "day in the life" description to her counselor, she was shocked to hear him accuse her of being codependent and enabling her husband's abusive behavior. In her outrage at such an accusation, she wrote to me, asking me if victims were codependent enablers who should be searching their hearts for their contribution to or responsibility in the abusive relationship.

This was my reply:

> No. The answer is absolutely no. Victims do not enable their abuser's behavior in the sense that the victim's actions produce the abuse. The proof of this is that no matter what a victim does in regard to changing their behavior, the abuser will continue to abuse. Why? Because abusers abuse. That is who they are, and abuse is what they do. This was very, very wrong for the counselor to lay upon you.

> Because this is abuse, couple's counseling is not a healthy prescription for your situation. All it does is affirm to the abuser

---

[156] Vernick, *The Emotionally Destructive Marriage*, p 124.

that YOU are at least partially to blame, and he will use what you say in the joint sessions against you.

Are there things that victims can do to strengthen their defense against an abuser? Yes. Like drawing firm boundaries, or like calling him on his tactics when you see them (though many victims simply cannot do these things with safety). But your counselor is using "enabling" in a causative sense. That is to say, the counselor is telling you that your "codependent" behavior is causing the abuse. That is not true. Abuse is "caused" by the entitlement mentality of the abuser. What the counselor is wrongly labeling as codependency is most probably more likely what we call the "fog" (confusion) of abuse and the fear of the abuser.

Marriage is to make you holy instead of happy?

> I allowed him to control my view of God. . . . Now, I'm allowing the church to do the same. I don't feel worthy enough to come to God. After all, I'm a woman.

Apparently based on the book by Gary Thomas *Sacred Marriage: What if God Designed Marriage to Make Us Holy More than Happy,*[157] Christians have chided those who have expressed fear and despair over an abusive marriage. Based on teachings such as this, they have said that God's goal for His children is not to be happy, but instead God is using their abusive marriages—even the abuse itself—to sanctify them, to make them holy.

John MacArthur tells the abuse victim that God will give her grace to endure the suffering and become a great prayer warrior.

> The Lord will protect you and teach you in the midst of the difficult time. Of course, pray for your husband, submit to him in every way you can, encourage him to seek advice and counsel from other biblically-knowledgeable men—and do everything

---

[157] Zondervan, 2002.

you can to heal the problems that cause him to be angry or abusive.[158]

This illogical reasoning is against Scripture and common sense. Satan told Christ in the wilderness temptation to throw Himself off the pinnacle of the temple because the Father promised to send angels to catch Him. We all know Jesus' response. "You shall not put the Lord your God to the test."[159] If the Lord puts us in a difficult spot, if He leads us into suffering for our good, then that is His doing. And there will not be, until He permits, a way of escape (think of Paul praying for the thorn in the flesh to be removed). But when there is a way of escape, we are free to take it. It is wrong, and I would say even arrogant, for any human being to pronounce to us that "the Lord has done this and put you here and He wants you to stay in this situation." That kind of advice is presumptuous and sounds like the simplistic theology of Job's friends.

More lies and more truth

Lie: A good woman can have a good marriage even if her husband is not a good man. A woman who truly desires to obey God is all a good marriage requires.[160]

Truth: A marriage is a covenant between a man and a woman. A good marriage requires two people, fulfilling their vows to each other. A bad marriage requires only one to break them.

Lie: "The atmosphere of the home is determined more by the mother and wife than by the father and the children. . . . Man doesn't determine the mood of the house; you do! You are the Holy Spirit of the home."[161]

Truth: Husband and wife (and children, if they are older) share responsibility for the atmosphere of the home. A positive, joyful

---

[158] John MacArthur, "Answering the Key Questions about the Family," Grace to You Website, http://www.gty.org/resources/positions/p00/answering-the-key-questions-about-the-family

[159] Matthew 4:5-7.

[160] Handford, *Me? Obey Him?* p 77.

[161] Jack Hyles, *Woman the Completer* (Hyles-Anderson Publishers, 1981), accessed via http://www.jackhyles.com/woman.htm

atmosphere in a home can be destroyed by an abuser. And no one is the Holy Spirit of the home except the Holy Spirit.

Lie: You have no rights until you do your job and submit to your husband. A wife bears more guilt when she doesn't submit than a husband bears when he doesn't love.[162]

Truth: Every person has God-given rights and deserves to be treated with dignity.[163] Respectful boundaries are absolutely appropriate in order to maintain that dignity.

Lie: If a husband is abusive, it is because his wife does not obey and honor him enough.[164]

Truth: If a husband is abusive, it is because he is an abuser. His wife will not be able to fix his abusiveness.

Lie: If a wife becomes more submissive, she can help her husband stop abusing.[165]

Truth: An abuser's repentance is his own responsibility before God. He needs to go to Christ to repent of his sin of abuse and to be transformed by Him from being abusive to be kind and loving.

Lie: God will never give you more than you can handle.

Truth: The Bible and history both show that God often allows people to be overwhelmed by more than they can "handle" in their own strength. This lie is probably based on I Corinthians 10:13, "No temptation has overtaken you that is not common to man. God is faithful, and he will not let you be tempted beyond your ability, but with the temptation he will also provide the way of escape, that you may be

---

[162] Ibid. See also DeMoss, *Lies Women Believe*, pp 73-76, where she states that "staking out" rights will cause a woman to be "moody, uptight, and angry."

[163] For more about our rights, see http://bjugrace.com/2015/03/03/replying-to-one-who-says-christians-should-have-no-rights/

[164] Debi Pearl, *Created to Be His Help Meet: Discover How God Can Make Your Marriage Glorious* (No Greater Joy Publications, 2014), p 79.

[165] Hyles, *Woman the Completer*.

able to endure it." Notice that this verse does *not* say that God will not give us more than we can handle in our own strength, but simply that He will provide a way of escape in the midst of temptation. These are two very different statements.[166]

Churches have failed

He screamed at me and my children, threatening to throw us out of the house if we didn't change. He screamed at me in front of my friend because I was disrespecting him by not doing what he thought I should do. He screamed whenever he thought the children or I had disrespected him.

Sometimes he wanted me to go to bed with him at eight pm and leave the middle-schoolers up by themselves. Sometimes he would push me out of the bedroom at bedtime and lock the door. Once he threw a coffee cup across the kitchen right past me, putting a big chip in our new sink. (He told me to fix the sink myself.)

He is six feet tall. I am five feet two. He would tower over me screaming, looking down on me, our bodies almost touching. Once I yelled back, so he hit me so hard with his chest that it sent me flying backwards onto the floor. He walked away, and I lay on the floor for a few minutes in shock.

About six months later it happened again. This time he got a look of rage in his eyes and grabbed my neck with both of his hands. I was petrified and thought it might be the end for me. After what seemed like an eternity, he loosened his grip and walked away. This incident was not spoken of either.

Another time when he shoved me in anger while we were arguing, I went flying backwards and hit my head on the floor. He started to come at me while I was on the floor. I yelled "Call the police," and my daughter called 911. He went outside and talked to the police calmly.

When my son was a freshman in high school, he did something that enraged [the abuser], who grabbed my son and yanked him to the floor. He had him pinned He had him pinned down and held his fist cocked back, screaming, "You want me to punch you, you want me to punch you!"

---

[166] More examples of unbiblical and unhelpful counseling include "God never wastes pain"; "If your husband needs a mother, then that is what God has called you to be"; and "Christ suffered more than you ever will, so don't complain." There are many others.

> *I moved out. I had had enough and I wanted better for my children and myself. I lost every penny I had in that marriage, hundreds of thousands of dollars. But God has blessed me with a few close friends and family who support me.*

This woman, like so many whose stories we have heard, was eventually excommunicated from her church for not reconciling with her abuser.

Church leaders have preached on the great doctrines of the faith, even preached them accurately. Church leaders have taught about marriage and husbands and wives, and even taught these truths accurately. But this wisdom and teaching has not gone far enough.

Preachers who love God have failed to paint a clear picture of abuse as sin. As a result, the abuser can easily dismiss the preaching as being about someone else. He can sit comfortably in his Sunday seat, wearing the effective mask of the saintly Christian, confident that his church loves him and will support him if his crazy wife ever tries to talk to anyone about how he exercises his "headship."

Church leaders have failed to understand the dynamics of abuse and have failed to listen to the words of their sermons through the ears of the abuser and the abused. Taking Scriptures out of context and applying them without understanding, Christian leaders and the Christian community at large have shown their arrogance and ignorance in counseling the victims.

When the church fails in this crucial matter, justice is perverted and evil wins. When the children grow up, all too often they turn from the family, the church, and the true God, not understanding that the god of this church was not the true God at all.

If one quality in every real Christian is a hunger and thirst for righteousness, how can true Christians pervert true justice and oppose true righteousness? This cannot be. So our words echo the words of Christ in Matthew 23: "Woe to you, scribes an Pharisees, hypocrites! Repent!"

CHAPTER 7

Is Domestic Abuse a Lifetime Deal?

Jesus and the apostles held a crystal clear position: marriage of one man to one woman for life is without question the model set before us. This has been God's plan from the beginning.

But the situation changes with the entrance of willful, habitual, unrepentant, hard-hearted, hypocritical sin. Because of this, abuse victims need to hear us plainly and confidently telling them two foundational assumptions, so that they can make wise decisions for their future. First, abusers do not change. What I mean by this is that cases of genuine, heart transformation of an abuser into not only a non-abuser, but into a person who actively loves the one they used to torment and works to expose abuse—such cases are so very rare that I believe it is unwise for an abuse victim to base her decisions and thinking on the hope that "maybe he'll change." [167] Such thinking will not lead to helpful

---

[167] One domestic abuse counselor said, "In my experience over the last six years working at [a domestic abuse shelter], I know of only one client out of hundreds whose abusive partner changed." She went on to describe the change: "[The former abuser's] wife reports that he actively works alongside her to expose characteristics and forms of abuse. She reports that he takes full responsibility to her and others for the abuse that he inflicted on her. She reports feeling safe and feeling like she has an equal voice in her home now. This isn't something that happened over night. He had to choose to put in a lot of personal work to transition his thinking and behavior from that of control and power to instead one of respect and love."

decisions and is almost always a setup for disappointment and further abuse.

Second, a marriage to an abuser does not need to be fixed, it needs to be ended, as this chapter will explain.

If an abuse victim files for divorce from her abuser, is she a sinner to be excommunicated from the church and handed over to Satan in order to be taught "not to blaspheme"? Or does Christ permit her to be free?

When a Christian in a domestic abuse situation begins to look for solutions, she usually reads books or blogs by respected Christians, talks to her Christian friends, or asks her pastor. Sadly, the confusion, and often even her suffering, are increased by what abuse victims are typically told. Of the hundreds of books on Christian marriage, out of the top ten most popular on Amazon during the writing of this chapter, seven of them either do not mention abuse at all or only give it a passing nod, deeming it, for example, "inappropriate." These books present some of the most typical teachings about divorce for abuse:

Divorce and Remarriage: A Permanence View, by Wingerd, Elliff, Chrisman, and Burchett[168] teaches no divorce for any reason. The authors, who are pastors, will bring church discipline upon those in their congregation who violate this position. In *This Momentary Marriage*,[169] author John Piper also says that the marriage covenant must be kept unilaterally, lest Christ be discredited in the eyes of the world.

In *The Divorce Dilemma: God's Last Word on Lasting Commitment*,[170] author John MacArthur maintains that divorce is permissible for adultery or for desertion by an unbelieving spouse. God's "last word," according to MacArthur, is that the victim of the evils of abuse that we've been learning about in this book is not justified in divorcing her tormentor. "Abuse is not a biblical cause for divorce. A woman may

---

[168] Christian Communicators Worldwide, 2009.
[169] Crossway, 2012.
[170] Day One Publications, 2009.

have to find shelter and protection through her church, but she has not been given the right by God to divorce her abuser."[171] On his Grace to You website, MacArthur is asked how to deal with "intolerable" marriage situations such as child molestation or wife beating. He claims that I Corinthians 7:10 says that if the wife divorces, she is to remain unmarried or be reconciled with her husband. Even if the abusive man has beaten or committed incest against the children, MacArthur says that there are no biblical grounds for divorce.[172]

The message of this book is different. When God's people have become enslaved to evil distortions of God-given institutions, then I submit that one of the most Christ-like things we can do is work to help set those people free.

God's law for the Sabbath . . . and for marriage

Jesus proclaimed that the Sabbath was made for man, not man for the Sabbath.[173] But to the Pharisees, the Sabbath became so exalted that man became its slave, with heavy burdens regarding its observance. This practice of "heaping grievous burdens"[174] on others was the very opposite of God's original intent for the Sabbath. A day of rest that anticipated the coming of our perfect rest in Christ's sacrifice was made into an oppressive tyrant. Jesus taught instead that the Sabbath is to be observed *for man's sake,* so that he might rest and refresh himself and enjoy God.

The Pharisees and scribes were, apparently, careful students of the Scriptures. And yet they completely missed the greater things, such as the Lord's desire for *mercy* even more than sacrifice. As a result, these scholars ended up misapplying the Word of God and condemning the innocent. In Matthew 12:7 Jesus told them, "And if you had known what

---

[171] John MacArthur, "Answering the Key Questions about the Family," Grace to You Website, http://www.gty.org/resources/positions/p00/answering-the-key-questions-about-the-family.

[172] John MacArthur, "Dialogue on Divorce," Grace to You website, www.gty.org/resources/sermons/2221/Dialogue-on-Divorce. Though this article is from 1979, it is still available through the GTY website, indicating that this is still the view that MacArthur espouses.

[173] Mark 2:27.

[174] From Matthew 23:4, King James Version.

this means, 'I desire mercy, and not sacrifice,' you would not have condemned the guiltless."

The reality is that, just like the Sabbath, people were not made for marriage, but rather, marriage was made for people.

Marriage is a gift created by God for men and women to enjoy, not an ordinance to which people are to be enslaved at all costs.

When Bible scholars minutely dissect the meaning of *porneia* or make one statement of Jesus into an absolute rule given to govern every situation (which He never intended it to be), they are neglecting God's greater principles, such as His desire for mercy and His desire for us to protect the poor and helpless. The welfare of the victim becomes subservient to the institution of marriage. This teaching is a tradition of man that has created a burden God never intended people to have to bear.

Under this teaching, the abuser doesn't have to pay the heavy price paid by the one who is being abused, a fact reminiscent of Jesus' words against the Pharisees: "They tie up heavy burdens, hard to bear, and lay them on people's shoulders, but they themselves are not willing to move them with their finger."[175] *The Message* gives the rendition of this verse this way: "[T]hey package [God's Law] in bundles of rules, loading you down like pack animals. They seem to take pleasure in watching you stagger under these loads, and wouldn't think of lifting a finger to help."[176]

It was not the Sabbath itself that Jesus opposed, but the twisted perversion of it that had been imposed upon people by the Jewish leaders. In the same way, it is not the blessing of marriage as created by God for our good that we oppose, but the wicked, twisted thing it becomes in the hands of evil people.

When God's people awaken to the real existence and nature of abuse, they will surely necessarily realize that we have been guilty of

---

[175] Matthew 23:4.
[176] *The Message* (NavPress, 2002), Matthew 23:4.

condemning the innocent and protecting the wicked, who are often incredibly deceptive.

When innocent victims are being told that they must remain with their abuser and suffer his evil no matter what, Christians are doing what Jesus forbids: withholding mercy and condemning the guiltless.

We ourselves will be guilty of demanding sacrifice rather than offering God's mercy to the weak and helpless.

The covenant of marriage

Two kinds of covenants

The Bible says that marriage is a covenant. For example, Malachi 2:14 says, "the LORD was witness between you and the wife of your youth, to whom you have been faithless, though she is your companion and your wife by covenant." Proverbs 2:17 also refers to marriage as a "covenant made before God."

Some Christians have believed and taught that a covenant is not the same thing as a contract and that, though a contract can be broken, a covenant cannot be.

But the Bible makes no such distinction between a covenant and a contract. Only one Hebrew word, *berith*, is used in the Old Testament to mean any solemn agreement between two people, between two people groups, between God and a man, or between God and a people group. Studying all of the almost three hundred occurrences of the word can tell us much about what this term means.[177] Every *berith* made by God's people, whether in business or in personal relationship, was considered a solemn, holy vow, and they called God to witness. This is what is meant by making a covenant "before the Lord." Jeremiah 34:8-16 tells the story of people who broke their covenant (or contract) by violating

---

[177] The New Testament word *diatheke* is usually translated *testament*, but (except for possibly Hebrews 9:16-17) it carries the same meaning of "solemn agreement" and would well be rendered *covenant*.

the vows they made before the Lord, going back on what they had solemnly agreed to do. This, in effect, was as if they had broken covenant with God Himself.

Two types of covenants can be found in the Bible: unilateral and bilateral. In a unilateral covenant, one party is bound, while the other has no commitment.[178] In a bilateral covenant, both parties must agree to meet the terms of the solemn vows that they both take before the Lord.[179] Each covenant/contract, whether unilateral or bilateral, comes with terms that must be met and often with sanctions (curses) if the terms are not met. Nehemiah 10:29 says that when the people of God swore an oath (covenant) before God to walk in His law, they "took on themselves a curse" if they did not keep it.

Marriage is a bilateral covenant

In a wedding ceremony, both parties take solemn vows (the terms of the covenant) in the presence of God and witnesses.[180] These vows that are recited at the wedding ceremony are the terms of the covenant/contract, and include promises to love, to honor, to cherish, to forsake all others, and to remain faithful until death.

You know how it goes, even though you might not have paid much attention to it on your own wedding day. The minister says something like this:

"_____, will you take this woman/man to be your wife/husband, according to the ordinance of God, in the holy bond of marriage, and will you pledge your faith to him/her, in all love and honor, in all duty and service, in all tenderness, to live with her/him, and cherish her/him, comforting and keeping her/him, and forsaking all others remaining true to her/him, as long as you both shall live?"

---

[178] The covenant that God made with Noah in Genesis 9 is an example of a unilateral covenant, sometimes called a "covenant of promise."

[179] An example of a bilateral covenant is the covenant made between Abraham and Abimelech in Genesis 21.

[180] If I am officiating at the wedding of a couple who want to write their own vows, I reserve the right to review what they have proposed. Because vows are solemn promises before God and witnesses, that they must state certain commitments that the husband and wife are making to each other.

Both marriage partners say, "I will." Then they repeat these words, or something similar:

"I, _____, take you, _____, to be my wedded wife/husband according to God's holy ordinance, and I do promise and covenant, before God and these witnesses, to be your loving and faithful husband/wife, to have and to hold, from this day forward, for better, for worse, for richer, for poorer, in sickness and in health, in joy and in sorrow, to love and to cherish, as long as we both shall live."

Some have indicated that the worse, poorer, sickness, and sorrow all include abuse, which would mean that a spouse will be violating the covenant to escape an abusive marriage. But is this true? Notice that each partner is promising to pledge faith, love, honor, duty, service, tenderness, cherishing, comforting, keeping, and forsaking others.

The hard times described in the vows, through which the two who have pledged to each other will continue in their faithfulness, are the hard times of life circumstances.

Breaking of the vows is not included—if it were, it should be clearly stated with words that commit to unilateral covenant-keeping, such as "and though you break faith, yet I will remain faithful." Those who believe in no divorce for any reason might want to insist on such words in the marriage vows, so that each marriage partner in such a church will have a clear understanding of what it is they're getting into.

The fact that the vows are recited in "the presence of God and these witnesses" acknowledges, as the London Confession of Faith states, God is being invoked to either bless or curse. It goes on to say, "Whoever takes an oath warranted by the Word of God, ought duly to consider the weightiness of so solemn an act, and therein to vow nothing but what he knows to be truth; *because by rash, false, and vain oaths, the Lord is provoked. . . .*"[181] Though the word *curse* is not used in the wedding vows, the husband and wife should both clearly understand that by taking

---

[181] 1689 London Confession of Faith 1689, chapter 23, paragraph 3.

these solemn vows they are calling down the curses of the Lord on themselves if they refuse to follow through.

A wedding is certainly cause for celebration, but many partying weddings might suddenly have a more sober atmosphere if the bride and groom were to say,

---

"Lord, we ask you to bless us or curse us according to how we keep the solemn vows we are now making."

What reasonable person would ever enter into a bilateral covenant/contract knowing that the other person can speak the words of the vow in utter deceit and then go on to violate the terms grievously and repeatedly, assured that the other party cannot acknowledge this breaking of the covenant? And yet many pastors and Christians today hold to such a low view of marriage that they are willing to say, "The marriage covenant states that you cannot divorce your spouse even if he is flagrantly breaking all those vows he made to you. You've got to put up with ill treatment no matter what. To do otherwise is to sin." They treat a bilateral covenant as if it is unilateral.

God's broken marriage covenant

Throughout the Old Testament, God compared His covenant with Israel, which the Israelites entered into at Mt. Sinai, to marriage. This covenant was bilateral, since both He and they solemnly agreed to its requirements. The violation of the bilateral agreement of that covenant/contract God called adultery. Ultimately, after much patient forbearing with the covenant-breaking of His people, the northern tribe of Israel, there came a point when God said, "Enough," and He divorced His bride.[182] In Jeremiah 3:8, God says that the southern tribe of Judah "saw that for all the adulteries of that faithless one, Israel [the northern tribe], I had sent her away with a decree of divorce."

Notice that the one who destroyed the marriage was Israel, not God. God was the one who was sinned against, the victim of broken vows.

---

[182] See also Hosea 9:15-17.

God Himself, who is incapable of sin, could be considered a divorcee.[183] If we charge that the victim of abuse who files for legal divorce because of the breaking of the marriage covenant is guilty of sin, then by extension we're charging God with sin, since His situation with Israel was the same. If God were to declare all divorce to be sin, then He would be condemning Himself.

What makes a covenant impossible to break?

The "permanence view" of marriage maintains that the marriage covenant cannot be broken except by death. Because of their lack of understanding of the bilateral nature of the covenantal agreement, those who hold to the permanence view do not allow for the violation of the marriage vows as legitimate grounds for dissolution of the marriage.

But in reality God's unilateral "covenants of promise" are the only covenants that are impossible to break, because He is the one meeting all of the terms.

The New Covenant in Christ is unilateral—one party, Jesus Christ, has all the responsibility, even while both parties benefit. The only reason this covenant is impossible to break is because the one who is fulfilling all the requirements of the covenant is one who cannot fail to accomplish this fulfillment. Jesus Christ was crucified for His people so that we could die in Him, and was raised for His people so that we can be raised in Him, to walk in newness of life.[184]

Jeremiah 31 and Ezekiel 16 both prophesy the coming of a New Covenant, when a new living heart will replace the old heart of stone in the people of God. Hebrews 8:7-10 refers to it again. God said of His New Covenant people, "I will be their God, and they shall be my people" because "I will put my laws into their minds, and write them on their

---

[183] See also Bronwyn Lea, "What God Teaches Us About Broken Marriage Vows," *Christianity Today,* February 27, 2014, acessed via
http://www.christianitytoday.com/women/2014/february/what-god-teaches-us-about-broken-marriage-vows.html
[184] Romans 6:4.

hearts." The Lord *will be* their God and they *will be* His people. There will be no divorce between Christ and His true bride, those who have put their trust in Him.[185]

In *Lies Women Believe,* author Nancy Leigh Demoss says, "Marriage is a lifelong covenant that is intended to reflect the covenant-keeping heart of God. As He is faithful to His covenant, so we must be faithful to keep our marriage covenant. . . . God's grace is sufficient to enable you to be faithful to your mate and to love and forgive without limit."[186] DeMoss clearly misses the fact that God's New Covenant is kept unilaterally by Him alone, as He Himself indwells our hearts to empower us. Or maybe DeMoss misses the fact that marriage is not a unilateral covenant, but a bilateral one.

How the marriage covenant can be broken

The "permanence view" of marriage can be held only by people who either are abusive themselves or are clueless regarding the real nature of covenants and the real nature of abuse.[187] Permanence-view Christians may be well-meaning in their zeal for God, but it is zeal without knowledge, and it is working great injustice and harm in the body of Christ.

Jesus did not teach the permanence view of marriage. He acknowledged that a separation could happen in a marriage by giving instruction in Matthew 19:6 (and in the parallel passage Mark 10:7-9) that because the two who are married have been joined by God to become one flesh, no man *should* separate, or put a division between

---

[185] The New Covenant is not made with the same "bride" as the Old. It is established with the Church, not with physical, earthly Israel.

[186] DeMoss, *Lies Women Believe,* p 163.

[187] In *Jesus and Divorce* (Wipf & Stock Publishers, 1984), authors Gordon Wenham and William Heth maintain that divorce is not permitted for adultery and that all remarriage is forbidden. Heth later changed his mind and accepted divorce for adultery and desertion, and, after reading *Not Under Bondage* by Barbara Roberts, he now accepts abuse as a ground for divorce. Heth's commendation for *Not Under Bondage* says, "This book removed the scales from my eyes and brought me face to face with the plight of victims of abuse."

them.[188] What Jesus forbids with these words is *the destruction of the marriage by violation of the vows.*[189]

The majority of conservative evangelical Christians would agree that adultery would destroy a marriage covenant/contract, according to Matthew 19:9, by a violation of the vow of faithfulness. In cases of adultery, the wronged party may choose to remain in the marriage but is not obligated to do so.[190]

I Corinthians 7:15 indicates that desertion is another way the marriage covenant can be destroyed.[191] The Westminster Confession of Faith says, "[N]othing but *adultery, or such willful desertion as can no way be remedied by the Church or civil magistrate,* is cause sufficient of dissolving the bond of marriage."[192] Physically leaving is one form of desertion. Causing the marriage partner to be forced to leave, for her health and safety (and that of her children), is another.[193]

When one marriage partner engages in willful, habitual, unrepentant breaking of the marriage vows, what was supposed to be a marriage has become a distorted, evil instrument of slavery.

---

[188] See also Roberts' discussion of the meaning of "what God has joined together," http://cryingoutforjustice.com/2013/11/06/isnt-adultery-the-only-ground-for-divorce.

[189] Two authors offer an excellent treatment of this passage: Barbara Roberts in *Not Under Bondage: Biblical Divorce for Abuse, Adultery and Desertion,* and David Instone-Brewer in *Divorce and Remarriage in the Church,* along with his *Divorce and Remarriage in the Bible.* These works provide the clearest and most accurate exposition of the central passages on marriage and divorce as seen in the cultural context in which they were written. Roberts' book is specifically written to address the common misuses of Scripture that continue to enslave victims in abusive marriages.

[190] Years ago I counseled a couple with a history of adultery by one of them, I said, "Your marriage was destroyed by the violation of your marriage covenant. Therefore the wronged party has the right to acknowledge this fact by filing the necessary legal papers with the civil court. You are not required to do so—you may choose to forgive and continue on in the marriage. But this is your right." In this case, the wronged spouse chose to forgive and continue in the marriage. Perhaps in cases like this it would be appropriate to recite new vows to establish a new covenant.

[191] I Corinthians 7:10-16 is dealt with at length later in this chapter.

[192] Westminster Confession of Faith, chapter 24, paragraph 7.

[193] Some Reformers and other godly people have considered abuse to be a form of desertion. See Roberts, *Not Under Bondage,* Appendix 2 on "Constructive Desertion." Also Ray Sutton, *Second Chance: Biblical Principles of Divorce and Remarriage* (Dominion Press, 1988), pp 12-14.

The abusive spouse is the one who has separated what God has joined together. The abuser has engaged in what we would call "constructive desertion."

When this evil conduct creates unbearable conditions, the victim is not the deserter and bears no blame.

[A] true marriage covenant requires a true and cordial consent from both parties to the terms of the covenant. . . . [I]n any marriage covenant, the bridegroom agrees to be a husband to the bride, i.e., to care for, to protect, to nourish, to remain faithful to her. If the bridegroom is not agreeing to this from the heart, he is not agreeing to this at all. . . . While he might appear to agree to the terms—verbal consent with every intention to the contrary—such a ceremony may constitute a marriage covenant in the eyes of man, but it cannot possibly be a true marriage covenant in the eyes of Him who searches heart and mind.

The victim has every right to question whether the abusive man in question is actually a husband. In God's eyes, he did not agree to the terms of the marriage covenant. From God's point of view, he is therefore not her husband. If she divorces this man, she may be consoled by the fact that there was no covenant of marriage to begin with. Abuse victims are often burdened with the pronouncement (and mistranslation of Scripture) "God hates divorce" (Malachi 2:16). But victims deserve to be consoled with the truth that God hates a certain kind of marriage—the kind of marriage that profanes his name due to false vows. She would also deserve to be consoled that she has every right to a second chance for a true covenant of marriage.[194]

---

[194] Dietrich Wichmann, "False Vows Do Not a Covenant Make," http://cryingoutforjustice.com/2014/10/22/false-vows-do-not-a-covenant-make-by-pastor-dietrich-wichmann.

After some time away, I knew leaving him was right, but I struggled with the actual divorce. I did not take my vows lightly. I began to search God's word on the topic. After a thorough study, I felt I was not going against the Bible by leaving or divorcing him, because my abuser had already broken the marriage covenant. Later, I discovered he had been cheating, so I had the backing of scripture on that as well. Still, I waited, wanting to be sure of God's will and God's timing. Eventually, my abuser indicated he wanted a divorce. I felt peace to proceed, and on the day my divorce was final I had a marriage certificate shredding ceremony.

During those four years in the house of horrors, I begged God not to let me go through the suffering without coming out ahead spiritually. I can thank my Lord Jesus Christ for answering that prayer. My faith truly became my own during that time of darkness, and ten years later I can praise the Lord I did not go through it in vain.

Defining divorce, really

When we speak of ending a relationship that an abuser might call "marriage," we need to remember that what is being ended is not really a true marriage. When the victim departs, she is merely acknowledging the fact that there is no marriage. The abusive spouse is actually not a husband, but an "anti-husband."[195]

I don't feel divorced. I feel like a widow. The truth is that the man I loved doesn't exist. I was in love with a lie. The abuser is the truth. The man I loved will never be; he never really was.

Once we recognize that marriage is a solemn covenant or contract, entered into with sober vows, we can define Biblical divorce, a term that isn't always as clear as some may think.

Biblical divorce is simply the legal declaration that a marriage, according to Biblical guidelines, is over because the contract has been negated and declared void.

[195] Credits to Ida Mae for the term "anti-husband," https://thoroughlychristiandivorce.wordpress.com/2012/02/09/you-married-a-what/

The abuse victim should not be obliged to wait interminably in hope that the guilty spouse may repent. Biblically, only the wronged party can decide when the marriage contract has been rendered null and void[196] and Biblically, only the wronged party can rightfully petition for divorce. When the wronged spouse takes the legal means to end the marriage (i.e., files for divorce with the civil authorities), this action is merely acknowledging that the marriage covenant has already been rendered void by the guilty spouse's violation of the covenant terms. In reality, all the victim is doing is bringing suit in order for the court to recognize that the marriage contract has already been broken. We even use that legal language—*suing for divorce.*

Victims of marital vow-breaking need to be assured that it is not a sin to divorce the guilty party.

When Christians insist that a victim who files for divorce is responsible for the destruction of the marriage, they are doing her great harm and injustice. The abuse victim who decides that the marriage has ended is not the one destroying the marriage. That has already been accomplished by the abuser, who has refused to love, honor, and cherish as he vowed before God to do. Instone-Brewer affirms this when he says,

> Therefore, although the breakup of a marriage is always due to sin, it is not the divorce itself that is the sin; the sin is the breaking of the vows, which causes the divorce.[197]

Imagine an abuser in the pre-marital stage with his mentality of entitlement to power and control, yet still hiding behind his façade of wool. Imagine if he were told these truths in marriage counseling. He would realize that his perfect façade is in danger of being exposed, and the church would no longer be a safe place to hide.

---

[196] Instone-Brewer, *Divorce and Remarriage in the Church,* Location 163, Kindle edition.
[197] Ibid., Location 160.

Sadly, though, many churches, while thinking that they are working to preserve marriages, are actively enabling abuse.

Some important Scriptures

Why did God say "I hate divorce"?

You may be surprised, but God didn't say this. When people bring up this objection, I ask them to show me the Bible verse. But they can't find those words unless they are using certain translations. Here is the verse, Malachi 2:16, in the ESV: "For the man who does not love his wife but divorces her, says the LORD, the God of Israel, covers his garment with violence, says the LORD of hosts. So guard yourselves in your spirit, and do not be faithless."

Why the disagreement among translators? My blogging partner from Australia, Barbara Roberts, explains it well on our blog, A Cry for Justice:

> Significantly, most people do not realize that Malachi 2:16, the text which has given rise to this saying, has been mistranslated. The incorrect translation came about as follows. The word *hates* in Malachi 2:16 is "he hates." The Hebrew denotes third person masculine singular = he. The King James version had, "For the LORD, the God of Israel, saith that he hateth putting away." Many subsequent translations switched the third person "he" to a first person "I" without any grammatical warrant. For example, the 1984 NIV was "'I hate divorce,' says the Lord God of Israel." Possibly translators thought the switch was okay because it retained the sense of the KJV—that God feels the hatred [for divorce]. They did not seem to worry that "I hate divorce" was grammatically inaccurate to the original Hebrew.[198]

> But this incorrectly-translated saying is now being bandied around like a proverb, dropped casually into sermons and

---

[198] Barbara Roberts, "God Hates Divorce? Not Always," accessed via http://cryingoutforjustice.com/2013/10/24/god-hates-divorce-not-always.

magazine articles, propounded in marriage manuals, amplified in Bible studies, and thrust accusingly over cyberspace and kitchen tables. It appears to condemn all acts of divorcing, with no thought for who is the innocent party. Christian victims of domestic abuse have it carved in stone in their minds and feel trapped between two terrible alternatives: stay in the marriage (and suffer the destruction of ongoing abuse), or reap condemnation for divorcing their abusive partners.[199]

But modern translations are starting to correctly this mistake. The construction in Hebrew ("he hates . . . he covers") shows that the one who feels the hatred is not God, but the divorcing husband. To be faithful to the Hebrew, the verse could be rendered, "If he hates and divorces,' says the Lord God of Israel, 'he covers his garment with violence.'" It is talking about a husband who hates his wife and divorces her because of his aversion for her. Therefore, Malachi 2:16 is only referring to a specific type of divorce: divorce for aversion, which could be dubbed "hatred divorce." Divorce for hatred is treacherous divorce: if a man hates his wife and dismisses her, he "covers his garment with violence" — his conduct is reprehensible, he has blood on his hands. . . . .

Malachi 2:16 does not condemn all divorce. It certainly does not condemn the divorce which a person might take out because of the persistent misbehavior of their spouse. It doesn't condemn divorces undertaken because of adultery, abuse or desertion.[200]

I Corinthians 7—living with an unbeliever

When Jesus in Matthew 19 allowed for divorce only for adultery, we know that He wasn't making a universally true, absolute law, because in I Corinthians 7 the Apostle Paul said that the Lord Jesus did not address

---

[199] A third alternative presented to the victim is almost as bad: separate from the abuser but never divorce—a state of limbo which still brings tongue wagging from the church and leaves the victim vulnerable to a dangerous reconciliation if an unreformed abuser makes an outward show of reformation.

[200] Barbara Roberts, "God Hates Divorce? Not Always," accessed via http://cryingoutforjustice.com/2013/10/24/god-hates-divorce-not-always.

the particular situation Paul was addressing. Each of the Scriptural passages that speaks to the issue of divorce should be taken in light of other passages on the topic, and all should be interpreted together.[201] In I Corinthians 7:10-15, under the inspiration of the Holy Spirit, Paul wrote:

> To the married I give this charge (not I, but the Lord): the wife should not separate from her husband (but if she does, she should remain unmarried or else be reconciled to her husband), and the husband should not divorce his wife.

> To the rest I say (I, not the Lord) that if any brother has a wife who is an unbeliever, and she <u>consents to live with</u> him, he should not divorce her. If any woman has a husband who is an unbeliever, and he <u>consents to live with</u> her, she should not divorce him. For the unbelieving husband is made holy because of his wife, and the unbelieving wife is made holy because of her husband. Otherwise your children would be unclean, but as it is, they are holy.

> But if the unbelieving partner <u>separates</u>, let it be so. In such cases the brother or sister is not enslaved. God has called you to peace.

Though a much fuller treatment of this passage can be found elsewhere,[202] the highlights of this text tell us that in verses 10-11 Paul addresses marriages in which both spouses are Christians. In verses 12-16, he is dealing with an issue that Jesus didn't mention ("I, not the Lord"), namely, a marriage between a believer and an unbeliever.[203] If

---

[201] Pastor David Dykstra offers a wise treatment of Luke 16:18 and Matthew 5:31-32 in his sermon "That Thorny Issue of Divorce," available at www.sermonaudio.com.

[202] See Instone-Brewer, *Divorce and Remarriage in the Church,* in particular his background for interpreting I Corinthians through an understanding of Exodus 21:10-11. Roberts, *Not Under Bondage,* also gives careful attention to this passage.

[203] This situation can arise because two non-Christians are already married, and one comes to faith in Christ while the other doesn't. However, another common scenario typical of abuse victims is that the abuse victim honestly believed that her abuser was a Christian when she married him and found out after the wedding that he wasn't. See Roberts, pp 40-41.

the unbeliever "consents to live with" the believer, the Christian is encouraged to remain in the marriage.[204]

The phrase used twice in verse 13, "consents to live with," should not be construed to mean simply inhabiting the same house. The Greek words being used here could be rendered "identifying closely, being of one mind, agreeing to dwell or abide together in a deep personal way." When Peter said in I Peter 3:7, "Likewise, husbands, *live* with your wives in an understanding way," he indicated in his use of a very similar Greek word that "to live with" means "to remain in the marriage, showing understanding and deference to one's spouse." If an unbeliever continues in the marriage in this way, honoring the marriage vows, then the Christian spouse has no grounds for divorce.

For abusers, though, it is *characteristic* to refuse to "consent to live with" their victim—to dwell in understanding and agreement and love[205]—but instead they thumb their noses at the marriage covenant, which includes their promise to love, cherish, and protect their partner.

The abuser as we have defined him is not a Christian.[206] Instead of consenting to live with the partner he vowed to love and cherish, he "separates" as verse 15 says, or detaches himself from the covenant, rendering it invalid.

The Christian is therefore not required to remain in this marriage in which she is treated worse than trash.

"Let it be so" tells the victim and the church to recognize and accept reality: the marriage has been destroyed, and the victim may obtain the certificate that gives legal recognition of this fact.

---

[204] Their children are considered "clean/holy" before God, because they would have more opportunity to come to faith in Christ than children of two unbelievers.

[205] Often at the same time they will claim that they don't want a divorce. This can be construed as an example of the crazy-making that an abuser commits, described in Chapter 3 of this book.

[206] No genuine believer walks in sin or is characterized by the evil mind that an abuser has. See Galatians 5:16ff; Romans 8; I John 2.

She is Biblically free to divorce, and she should not be condemned for doing so.

In a heart-moving letter to the church I pastor, Christ Reformation Church in Oregon, an abuse survivor wrote to us to tell us her story and to thank us for helping her to freedom through our blog ministry and books. She had found freedom and peace in understanding that the abuser was the one who destroyed her marriage.

> *Without your encouragement and prayers and all that you do for those of us you've never met—well, all the evil dynamics I have told you about would still be in full force under the same roof. The abuser hasn't changed, and we are not yet fully divorced, but it's better now that we're no longer together. We are in the process of mediation and I know now that there can be no settling with the powers of darkness, so I am trusting the Lord for His deliverance in His time and His way. I have learned to shake the dust off my feet and move on.*

The "high view" of marriage

Who has the highest view?

For the most part, the church tells people that none of the promises their spouse made at the altar, except for physical faithfulness, can be enforced. Unlike *every other human contract/covenant*, it seems that the church believes that this covenant/contract can be disregarded and violated in a myriad of ways, even immediately after the wedding, with full immunity from sanctions (penalties, curses) and continued enjoyment of all privileges. A spouse can, for example, never love, never honor, never cherish the wife or husband, and yet we tell the wronged party that there is nothing that can be done about it. The defrauded party is still bound by contract/covenant to continue to live with the offending party. Those who espouse this view call it having a "high view" of marriage.

But who really holds to a high view of marriage? Those who insist that divorce is never permissible for abuse, and who therefore say that a marriage can still be a marriage when an abusive spouse is violating the marriage covenant vows every single day? Or those who say that those vows must be kept and that a "marriage" where there is abuse is in fact no marriage at all in God's sight?

In actuality, those who claim that abuse does not destroy/break the marriage covenant are the ones who have a low view of marriage. Or maybe they're making marriage into an idol.

Where the no-divorce for abuse position will lead

Pastor John Piper is one well-respected leader who teaches that the ultimate purpose of marriage is to display the glory of God and the covenant-keeping love between Christ and His church.[207] Because of this, he says, a victim of a domestic abuser is called to persist in keeping the marriage covenant as if it is a unilateral one.

This teaching can lead to absurd injustices. A woman who has been subjected to domestic terrorism for years, beaten and prostituted and sodomized by her "husband," whose children have been similarly tormented, is told that God does not permit her to declare her marriage void on the grounds of violation of the covenant. If she files for divorce from the wolf in sheep's clothing who has violated his marriage vows and instead marries a man who truly loves God and loves her and her children, the consummation of the new marriage will be considered an act of adultery.

Under this teaching, the victim in an abusive marriage who wants to follow Christ will struggle with a burden of guilt and despair as she believes that the only escape from her abuse is to hope and pray that either she or her abuser will die. The more committed she is to following Christ, the greater her guilt and hopelessness will become.

The abuser, on the other hand, hears that his victim is bound to him for life, regardless of whether or not he keeps the vows that he made in the marriage covenant. In his twisted thinking he can conclude, "Just what I knew! I am entitled and justified."

---

[207] John Piper, *This Momentary Marriage* (Crossway Books, 2009), p 42.

It seemed like many of the people in my life (pastors, family) who were pressuring me to "save the marriage at any cost" valued marriage itself more than . . . my safety and that of my children. I was told that women and children all over the world suffer all kinds of abuse at the hands of men and they survive it and their kids turn out okay, so I should be willing to do the same. I know now that their biggest problem was a misunderstanding of who God is. Marriage in effect became an idol as they asked me to be "holier" than God himself.

What about frivolous divorce?

I realize that some who call themselves Christians are far too liberal in permitting divorce for any reason. Serious-minded Christ-followers are rightly concerned about the epidemic of divorce that we see in Western culture. If we tell people that they can divorce when they believe their spouse has broken the wedding vows, they think, where will it end? And who ever really keeps the wedding vows perfectly anyway?

Even though Christ permits divorce when the marriage covenant is broken, we are never commanded or required to do so. Jesus emphasized the importance of forgiveness, loving our enemies, and not seeking vengeance when we're wronged. We know then that for any marriage to work, both partners must be quick to forgive one another.

However, the fact is most victims of abuse have made many efforts, even for *decades,* to seek to bring to repentance their hard-hearted, unrepentant perpetrator, who is wearing a "Christian" mask and duping the rest of us. They have sought help from pastors and other professionals. In many cases the victims have already borne too much for too long, and the pattern of abuse, the constant violation of the marriage covenant, has become deeply entrenched.

The solution to the cavalier disregard that some hold for the solemnity of the marriage vows is not to be found in racing to the other extreme that says divorce is never allowed.

The welfare of the victim and the solemnity of the vows must be held as more important than the institution of marriage.

Isn't it better for children to have both parents in the home?

Without a doubt the ideal for children is to have both a father and a mother. In non-abusive divorce cases, it makes sense to seek to provide children time with both parents. But treating a situation with an abusive spouse the same way can be not only foolish, but dangerous. This experience of one abuse survivor with her children is a common one:

> I have four children, same father, two adults and two still school aged, with a large gap between the two sets of kids. Two grew up with father and mother in the house. The other two are growing up in a "broken" home. Before the divorce, as God was leading me to it and I was greatly struggling with it, I cried out to Him that I would stay, even if it killed me, before I would harm those kids by leaving (the effects of exactly the kind of propaganda you are talking about). I struggled with Him for hours, more than once. He assured me that the divorce would be for the good of my kids as well as for my good. Eventually, I was at the place where I could move forward with divorce. That was a few years ago.
>
> Guess what? I am watching God fulfill what He promised me in regards to all of us! Among other things, my younger kids are learning how to deal with conflict, recognize manipulation, and live in the freedom of being who God created them to be. . . . I can see how my children who live in the "broken" home are becoming emotionally/relationally healthier than my children who grew up in the "unbroken" home. They will have less to overcome and heal from as adults than the rest of us. And God has graciously given me some glimpses of the positive effects of my divorce on my older kids as, it seems to me, not so much is taken for granted in their relationships, and they are working harder at them.[208]

Leave your church

Suppose a man was slowly poisoning his wife and children. You know that he's doing it, and you see the symptoms in his family members. You know that if it isn't stopped, ultimately they'll die.

What would you do? Would you tell the one who is being poisoned that God requires her to stay married, to submit and be more obedient so he would stop poisoning her?

---

[208] Comment on A Cry for Justice, www.cryingoutforjustice.com.

Would you recommend or even write books saying that the Bible prohibits divorce in cases of poisoning, and if the woman divorces her husband for the poisoning, she'll be in sin?

Maybe you would deny the evidence of poisoning and tell her that she's just imagining it, because "such a nice man" would obviously never do such a thing.

Maybe you would tell her that this poisoning is a trial that God has brought into her life to make her a better Christian, so she just needs to endure and trust the Lord, because marriage isn't about being happy and healthy, but is about being a living sacrifice.

Just so, when Christians tell victims to stay in an abusive situation, they are assigning them to die a slow, painful death, from the poison of abuse.

> I have to ask as a God-fearing, Bible loving Christian . . . when is enough enough? After two decades of a wife and children suffering actual physical harm, verbal and emotional abuse, thousands of broken promises, countless lies, being deprived of the most basic human needs even when it was in the husband's power to grant them, and the wife enduring repeated literal sexual assault, public and private humiliation, and endless, suffocating fear . . . when is it enough? Is it enough when your body starts to fail? When you become riddled with chronic stress-related disease? How about when you live for over five years waking up several times every night with night terrors?
>
> Well, my pastor said, knowing all of this, that God demands reconciliation with my husband or nothing. There are no other options. For my pastor, enough is never enough.

Though the no-divorce-for-abuse teachers may have a zeal for the Lord, if we consider abuse as defined and described in this book, we have to conclude that their teaching is spiritual malpractice. Exercising church discipline against abuse victims compounds this injustice. Surely this is abhorrent in God's sight.

I don't say this lightly, but I must say it for the welfare of abuse victims: I encourage any victim of abuse who is in a church that binds people in such a manner to leave that church for her own safety, sanity, and health. She needs to find a church that does not make the error of going beyond Scripture, but instead will help guide her through the difficult decisions she'll need to make, with understanding, compassion, and mercy.

> *I was forced to leave my home church over my refusal to "submit harder" to my abusive husband. Divorce is not permitted in my new church either, despite the fact that my husband is totally unrepentant. I feel like your book is a life line.*[209]

---

[209] Comment on A Cry for Justice, www.cryingoutforjustice.com.

CHAPTER **8**

Bringing the Charade to an End

Is the abuser a Christian?

> *And, finally, that brings up the uncomfortable issue of who is a real child of God and who is not. In addition to one's profession, according to I John, the acid test seems to be love. I don't think a person has to be perfect to be a believer, but it seems that if a wife or husband despite their profession and how many hours they spend listening to sermons, reading the Bible, and going to church, and yes, even involved in various ministries in the church, behave like they hate their spouse over a lengthy period of time, the reality of their relationship with God could be questioned. It is not my place to make that determination because I can't really know, nor can anyone really know, can they? And yet ... the fruit. ... So that is why this question is important in determining how to proceed with the relationship.*

It is common for Christian authors of marriage books and Christian leaders in churches to assume that the faithful church-attending, seemingly "normal" abuser—one such as what is described in this book— is a real Christian, a truly regenerated, new creation in Christ. They believe that helping him to stop abusing will be a process of helping him become more godly by helping him change certain habits.[210]

But is he actually even a Christian? How we view the answer to this question will have a profound effect on how we try to deal with the

---

[210] For example, see Jay Adams, *Godliness Through Discipline* (P&R Publishing, 1983), which clearly asserts that godliness can be achieved through development of habits.

abuser. Is he really a struggling saint who just needs to better understand who he is in Christ? Or is his Christianity an unholy charade?

When Christ saves us, He gives us a new heart. We are changed from hostility toward God to love for God, for His Word, and for others, especially those who belong to Christ. Any Christian can mistreat another person, but he will be like King David when Nathan the prophet came to him, truly repenting when confronted with his sin.

Too many Christians hold to a simplistic definition of Christianity: belief in a certain set of prescribed doctrines, and agreement to try to accomplish a certain list of prescribed duties. But every other religion in the world has these two stipulations. This is not the heart of Christianity.

Too many Christians judge a person's Christianity by his outward appearance and list-keeping actions. Is he faithful in attending church? Check. Does he pray a public prayer that gets many a resounding "Amen"? Check. Does he go "soul-winning"? Check. Does he praise the preacher? Check. Does he dress right and keep his hair cut a certain way? Check. And on and on the list goes, never ever investigating the heart of the matter—*does he truly love God and love others.*

Too many Christians believe that the entrance to God's kingdom is through praying the "sinner's prayer," which isn't even in the Bible. They then assure the one who prays that he is never to doubt his salvation, which effectively offers an open door to the abuser: "You are most welcome here."

What makes real Christianity different is the transformation that has taken place in the life of the one who has personally come to Christ.

Salvation in Christ changes our eternal destiny, but it also changes much more. True salvation changes the very essence of our personhood. Understanding what a true Christian is will revolutionize how we deal with abusers. A true Christian is:

- Once an enemy of God, one who is now His child who loves Him.[211]
- A new creature, a new man, a son of God.[212]
- One who has God's law written on his heart.[213]
- One who has been taught by the Spirit of Christ.[214]

In an abuser—with his utter self-centeredness and justification of his wrong actions, his lack of love for others and mindset of entitlement—all of these characteristics shout out loud that it is impossible for him to be a real Christian. Scripture clearly states that a person who lives for entitlement, power, control, and justification, is not in Christ, and Christ is not in him.[215]

If an abuser is treated as a real Christian who simply falls and struggles rather than as a person who has never known Christ, then the victim and other Christians will be confused about what it means to be a Christian. They will be led to think that abuse does not represent the abuser's true character, when in fact it does. The abuser himself will be escorted on his way to hell with his church's glib assurance that he really is a child of God.

In God's sight, if our churches continue to allow the abuse, we are in danger of having *Ichabod*, "the glory is departed,"[216] written over the doorposts of our churches every Sunday that we allow these master deceivers to continue to sit in our pews and stand in places of authority.

Shining the light of truth on abuse and abusers

When Jesus stood up in a public place and cried out in very specific terms the abuses that were being wreaked by the Pharisees, He publicly shone the light on sin. In this book and on our blog we are providing a

---

[211] I John 4:19; Galatians 4:4ff.

[212] II Corinthians 5:17; Ephesians 2:1ff.

[213] Hebrews 8:10-11.

[214] Ephesians 4:20ff.

[215] Romans 8:5 "For those who live according to the flesh set their minds on the things of the flesh, but those who live according to the Spirit set their minds on the things of the Spirit." Also see Romans 8:9; Ezekiel 36:26-27; Ephesians 2:10.

[216] I Samuel 4:21.

platform for abuse victims to publicly state what their abusers have done to them, in the context of explaining the mentality and tactics of abusers, and offering hope.

The most appropriate place for the dark evil of abuse to be exposed, though, is in the pulpits of our churches.

Christians must stop being squeamish and instead be willing to hear and read the testimonies of victims of domestic abuse in order to understand what abuse victims have to live with day in and day out.

His foul, stinking language and sickeningly mocking tone of voice. His perverse, pornographic sexual abuse. His threats of violence. His actual violence. All of it needs to be dragged out where everyone can see it.

Hold to a Christ-like view of sin

One of the first steps God's people can take is to remove the blinders about sin and wickedness. Do we understand how deceptive hypocrisy can be? Do we understand that abusers won't necessarily look evil to those of us on the "outside," but will often look like some of the nicest and wisest men of the church? Do we understand what the Bible teaches about sin? Do we understand that not all sins are equal and that not all sinners should receive equal punishment? Do we understand how the Lord views abuse, and do we hold the same attitude He does about the weak and helpless and those who abuse them? Are we making marriage an idol so that in our minds it comes before the safety and well-being of innocent people?

> *There it was—right in the middle of the I Corinthians 5 passage, one of the places my husband always turned to in order to justify his increasingly extreme definitions of Biblical separation. There in verse 11, among the people we were supposed to avoid, along with the infamous fornicator and the debated covetous—there was the Railer.*
>
> *I looked it up in Webster's 1828 dictionary. It was the kind of definition that struck deep and true. To rail was "to utter reproaches; to scoff; to use*

insolent or reproachful language; to reproach or censure in opprobrious ('reproachful and contemptuous') terms."

Was it really true? Did God really want us to be able to escape from those who claimed to be Christians but spoke with scorn and contempt, who scoffed and derided with reproachful and contemptuous language? That was how he spoke to us and treated us all the time.

After all the years of being taught that obedience to God allowed no way out, it seemed almost too unreal to be true. But there it was. It became the first real lifeline we discovered and clung to on our journey to break free.

Acknowledge the sin in the church

Cornelius Plantinga refers to some churches as having "tranquilized [their] spiritual central nervous system."[217] In such an environment, sociopaths will thrive. When we deny that such an evil could possibly be among us, then we are living as fools, the very kinds of fools the book of Proverbs warns about.[218] As the Pharisees exalted their own traditions over the authority of Christ, so can the modern-day people of God.

American churches far too easily point the finger at sin "out there," outside the church, instead of looking at the sin disguised behind the masks sitting in our pews. As long as this continues, abuse will increase.

Christians in our churches, and especially pastors, must stop covering their eyes and ears and playing "see no evil, hear no evil" within the body.

It is no denial of who Christ is or what He is accomplishing to acknowledge that this sin—the sin of abuse—can masquerade among us. Rather, it is a clear affirmation of everything the Bible tells us about the battle we as Christians have undertaken. When we confront a wolf in sheep's clothing, we are living the life of Christ.

---

[217] Cornelius Plantinga, *Not the Way It's Supposed to Be: A Breviary of Sin* (Wm. B. Eerdmans Publishing Company, 2010), Location 144, Kindle edition.

[218] Proverbs 13:16 says, "In everything the prudent acts with knowledge, but a fool flaunts his folly."

> *In church we were going over the Ten Commandments and I could not help but think about the second commandment . . . you are to have no other gods before me. It is hard to not have a god (abusive husband) before God sometimes, as you're walking on eggshells or in fear. The character of abuse does not match up with God's character. I am glad there are pastors and others who have allowed God to reveal so much to them to support victims and not let them feel forgotten, condemned to live a life with an abusive spouse.*

Prepare for reports of abuse

From the lessons we've learned at www.cryingoutforjustice.com, here are some guidelines for those in positions of leadership in churches.

- Understand that any kind of abuse is to be taken very seriously. Establish in your heart and mind that justice and protection for victims must be priority.
- Recognize that any person, no matter how affable, well-respected, or spiritually superior he seems, can be guilty of abuse. Plan ahead of time to refuse to be a respecter of persons.
- Before allegations of abuse arise, form alliances with local domestic violence shelters, rape crisis centers, and counseling centers.[219]
- When listing examples of sin in sermons and other venues, regularly mention abuse. This is a way of shining light on the sin.
- Pray publicly for victims and survivors of abuse. This will let victims know that it is safe to speak to you about their abuse, and it will let your congregation know where you stand.

Preach against abuse

When Christians, and especially pastors, are intimately familiar with the mentality and tactics of abusers, we will more effectively be able to expose the sin before the eyes of the abuser. Only when the abuser sees his own lost condition can he know how desperately he himself needs the gospel of Christ.

---

[219] Sadly, secular professionals are often more knowledgeable about domestic abuse than Christians are. But we highly recommend the work of Steven Tracy at www.mendingthesoul.org.

> *I think that often pastors preach sermons that are aimed to "strike the sinful person right between the eyes," but because it's being preached to the congregation as a whole, the abusers brush it off thinking it doesn't apply to them, while victims take it far too much to heart, scrutinizing and condemning themselves because of their over-sensitive consciences. Many times I sat beside my husband in church, examining myself scrupulously for every particular sin that the sermon was warning about, while my thick-skinned husband seemed to believe that none of the sermon's warnings applied to him.[220]*

If a pastor does speak from the pulpit about abuse in the church of Jesus Christ, he will elicit a variety of responses. Some will express their gratitude, even secretly, that the topic is finally being addressed. Some won't say anything but will show through their facial expressions that the topic fills them with fear and confusion. Some will be shocked, and will let you know that they believe this is not an appropriate topic for church.

And the abusers in the congregations? They'll be filled with "righteous indignation."[221] Sometimes against the speaker, but even more often against "those men" who would "dare" to do such a thing as abuse. I've found that this isn't always just a put-on, either. Abusers don't see themselves as abusers. It's "the guy who doesn't have justification like I do" who is the abuser.[222]

These reactions are all to be expected by those who are prepared. But we must press forward in exposing the truth. The evangelical, Bible-believing church has been rendering injustice to victims of abuse and enabling wicked, abusive people to continue in their secret reign of terror. It's time for that unholy charade to end.

Changes in your church

Your preaching will start to shake things up in your church. You will be opposed by abusers who have been hiding. You will be told to back

---

[220] Crippen and Wood, *A Cry for Justice*, p 257.

[221] Just as King David was when the prophet Nathan told the story about the lamb who was taken away from the poor man, in II Samuel 12.

[222] Bancroft, *Why Does He Do That?* p 158-159.

off by people who claim you are unjustly targeting them. You will suffer. Your church may even be split. Going up against the enemy's favorite strongholds is always an intense battle.

Something else will happen as well. Darkness that has been hidden for a long, long time will be brought to light. Victims of abuses will begin to come out of the bondage they have been held in for so long. Hypocrites will have to repent or "go out from among us, because they were not of us."[223] The weak and oppressed will begin to sense hope once again. In other words, the unholy charade will end. And only the Lord Himself knows what else He might do among you once the darkness is dispelled by the light of the truth of Christ. How many hidden things in our churches are quenching the Spirit of Christ and preventing Him from breaking out among us in revival?

Confronting the abuser

I believe that because abuse is a scandalous sin in the church, committed by a person who claims to be a Christian, that the best approach for confronting it is that of I Corinthians 5 rather than Matthew 18.[224] Knowing what you now know about the mentality and tactics of abusers, how will you confront him? [225]

Handling a report of abuse

- When a charge of abuse comes, believe the victim.[226] Resist any impulse to believe that the one making the accusation is the real abuser.

---

[223] I John 2:19.

[224] Barbara Roberts has written about the dangers of applying the Matthew 18 process to abusers. See http://cryingoutforjustice.com/2013/10/04/church-discipline-and-church-permission-for-divorce-how-my-mind-has-changed.

[225] If the victim is still living with the abuser, she could be put in great danger if you confront him. Make sure that when you do confront him, it is with her permission and in a way that will be safe for her.

[226] This is not to say that absolutely every accusation is true. But the problem in our churches has not been that we have been too gullible in believing false allegations. The problem has been that we have failed to believe victims who are speaking the truth. Shame and fear hinder victims from speaking, so that when they finally do, it is vital that they be believed. In all my years of listening to many, many abuse allegations, I have heard only two that ultimately proved to be false.

- Remember that wolves in sheep's clothing are everywhere. Resist the fear and denial that may come with the naming of the accused.
- Resist any impulse to think it can be handled quickly and quietly. (Always, however, consider the safety of the victim. In many cases it may not be wise to let the abuser know that his victim has reported the abuse to you.)
- Report the accusation to law enforcement, and allow them to deal with the accused.[227] Think of the civil authorities as those whom God has placed in these positions for our good.
- Do not ask for special treatment for the accused. Resist any urge to sit on the side of the accused in the courtroom.
- Let your congregation know about the situation. Protect the victim from accusations as much as possible. Warn church members to refrain from pressuring the victim to offer quick forgiveness and reconciliation.
- Accept the fact that you may be criticized for doing right. Seek justice, love mercy, walk humbly with your God, and then let the chips fall where they may.

A church that refuses to ignore abuse may be smaller in numbers, but will be stronger in righteousness.

Questioning his relationship with Christ and others

If a report of abuse is made to you against someone that you thought was a good man of the church, you now know to question his very relationship with Christ. As you listen to his answers to questions such as the following, you can look for the mentality of entitlement and justification. Though a genuine abuser may try to present the illusion of empathy and other positive character qualities, his tactics should become obvious as you listen, remembering that one of the most important tactics is the pity play, as will be described in the next section.

---

[227] Laws require pastors, as mandatory reporters, to report domestic violence incidents to the police if those incidents rise to the level of a crime as defined by the civil law (such as physical assault).

General questions[228]

- How can you make a righteous judgment as to whether someone else is a Christian? (If the person says, "I can't. Only God knows the heart," this is a red flag. Jesus said that by their fruit we shall know them. The "fruit" is not a certain kind of outward righteousness, but the fruit of the Spirit described in Galatians 5:22-23, which shows in works of love and kindness.)
- How long can a person persist in the same kind of sin and still be considered a Christian?
- What does it mean to repent?
- What does it mean to forgive?
- What is a woman's role in a marriage?
- What would cause a man to physically hurt his wife in some way?
- Is it right for a wife to spend money without first discussing it with her husband? Is it right for a husband to spend money without first discussing it with his wife?
- Give some examples of how children should show respect to their father. What kind of discipline is appropriate for a father to use on his children?
- What kind of discipline is appropriate for a husband to use on his wife?

Your personal life

- Describe your relationship with Christ. (Listen especially for any life changes he may describe, whether they are true fruit of the Spirit, or simply habits.)
- How does your Christianity affect your view of pornography? Lying? Obeying the law?
- What kinds of things cause you to become upset? What happens when you get upset?
- How do you handle arguments? When an argument is your fault, what do you do? How do you handle the situation when an argument is over? In general, do you handle arguments well?

---

[228] These questions are written to expose male abusers, and can be revised for female.

- How do you show repentance when you have failed?
- If you have been sinned against through word or deed, how do you react? What is our obligation to forgive?
- When you sin against someone else through word or deed, what is their obligation to forgive?
- If you have been married before, why did those marriages end? What kinds of women were those wives? What explanation would they give for the ending of the marriage?

Your relationship with your wife and children

- What do you think Biblical submission and obedience mean in the context of a marriage? Do you consider your wife to be Biblically submissive and obedient? Explain.
- What are your wife's obligations to you? How is your wife carrying out those obligations? What could your wife do to make your marriage better?
- What are your obligations to your wife? Give some examples of how you have lived out your obligations. How are you loving your wife as Christ loved the Church?
- Does your wife have any complaints about you? Which complaints do you think are true and fair?
- Does your wife ever misunderstand your motives? Give an example.
- What does your wife do to make you upset? How does she feel when you get upset?
- How does your wife handle arguments? When an argument is her fault, what does she do? How does she handle the situation when an argument is over? In general, does she handle arguments correctly?
- Does your wife usually think clearly? Give some examples of her primary thinking patterns as you perceive them.
- Does your wife have too many friends, or the wrong friends? Do you think they are causing problems in your marriage? How?
- What does it mean to raise your children in the nurture and admonition of the Lord? How are you doing that?

As you become more familiar with abuse, you can design follow-up questions to further reveal the mentality and tactics.

Remember an abuser's ability to lie

People who have never abused and have never been abused can have great difficulty grasping the way an abuser thinks (which is why this book was written!). After you have received an accusation and you are questioning him with the questions above, remember that real abusers can equivocate with absolute confidence.

Because abusers are often adept at telling convincing stories, they often have no true story to help them keep the facts straight.[229] As the person you are questioning expresses discrepancies in the telling of his story from one meeting to the next, you can record these and later press for more details or explanations. An abuser often can provide none.

Remember the pity play

Besides his other tactics, the abuser is usually very adept at eliciting sympathy and pity through his detailed, convincing stories and his expression of strong emotions, even weeping. His act may also include a show of fear of the victim, attempting to make her out as the abuser. It is crucial that you keep this pity play in mind as you deal with a person who has been accused of being an abuser.

> After listening for almost twenty-five years to the stories my patients tell me about sociopaths who have invaded and injured their lives, when I am asked, "How can I tell whom not to trust?" the answer I give usually surprises people. The natural expectation is that I will describe some sinister-sounding detail of behavior or snippet of body language or threatening use of language that is the subtle give-away. Instead, I take people aback by assuring them that the tip-off is none of these things, for none of these things is reliably present. Rather, the best clue is, of all things, the pity play. The most reliable sign, the most universal behavior of unscrupulous people is not directed, as

---

[229] In *Danger Has a Face* (Outskirts Press, 2011), author Anne Pike gives many examples of this phenomenon.

one might imagine, at our fearfulness. It is, perversely, an appeal to our sympathy. . . .[O]ur emotional vulnerability when we pity is used against us by those who have no conscience.[230]

"The most reliable sign, the most universal behavior of unscrupulous people is not directed, as one might imagine, at our fearfulness. It is, perversely, an appeal to our sympathy."
–Martha Stout

What does the Scripture say about pitying an abuser?

But if anyone hates his neighbor and lies in wait for him and attacks him and strikes him fatally so that he dies, and he flees into one of these cities, then the elders of his city shall send and take him from there, and hand him over to the avenger of blood, so that he may die. **Your eye shall not pity him,** but you shall purge the guilt of innocent blood from Israel, so that it may be well with you. [231]

Let's paraphrase this Scripture to apply it to our current issue:

If anyone hates his wife and sets traps for her and attacks her and strikes her so that her health is ruined and over time she sees herself dying, and he runs off to another church, the elders of his first church shall contact the elders of the church to which he has fled and he shall be put out of both churches, handed over to the Lord for the destruction of his flesh. **You shall not pity him,** but you shall purge your church from him, lest your entire church share in the guilt of innocent blood, so that the Lord will bless you and it might be well with you.

If an abuser succeeds in gaining pity,
he can get away with anything.

---

[230] Stout, *The Sociopath Next Door,* p 107. Stout goes on to describe an imprisoned sociopath that she interviewed whose greatest desire in life was to garner pity.

[231] Deuteronomy 19:11-13.

Do not fall prey to becoming one of the allies an abuser is constantly seeking.[232] Remember to keep your head on straight, accept no excuses or blaming of others, and do not pity an abuser, no matter how good an actor he may be.

You shall not pity him! Stop being swayed by the tears of the wicked. If you pity him, you will enable him.

You shall not pity him! To pity him is to keep him in your midst, and in doing so, everyone in that church will stand guilty before the Lord of the wicked man's evil, with innocent blood on their hands.

You shall not pity him! If you pity the wicked and harden yourself against the righteous ones who are oppressed by the wicked, God Himself will stand against you.

> *My pastors are constant targets of his attempts for pity as well. He texts them and says things about how he really desires to have a relationship with his children, but he just doesn't know how anymore because his wife has turned them against him, and how his wife refuses to go to counseling with him and won't try to reconcile. Those pastors have been very supportive of my decision to separate from my abuser. I suppose they do pity him, but not for the reasons he thinks.*

These words from Psalm 69 are a prophecy of the Lord Jesus Christ suffering on the cross, but they also speak of any abuse victim, accurately describing her painful plight:

Reproaches have broken my heart, so that I am in despair.

I looked for pity, but there was none, *and for comforters, but I found none.*[233]

God knew the ironic tendency of people to pity the evildoer and offer no pity for the one who is oppressed. But He also said that He

delivers the needy when he calls,

the poor, and him who has no helper.

He has pity on the weak and the needy,

---

[232] In *Danger Has a Face*, p 52, author Anne Pike also notes that the conscienceless person preys especially on those who are naïve and emotionally immature to be his allies. In other words, those who are as harmless as doves, but not as wise as serpents. See Matthew 10:16.

[233] Psalm 69:20.

and saves the lives of the needy.
From oppression and violence he redeems their life,
  and precious is their blood in his sight.[234]

We do have One who hears our cry. The One who does not pity the wicked has great treasures of pity for the righteous. Let us be like Him.

Follow Nathan's example

When the prophet Nathan told King David a story of a rich man who had stolen and killed a poor man's pet lamb, King David was incensed and proclaimed that the rich man should die. [235] He was quick to condemn one who had killed a lamb when he himself had been guilty of committing adultery and killing the husband of the woman he had compromised.

But then Nathan cried out, *"You are the man!"* Suddenly David understood and then saw himself in the mirror of Nathan's story. He repented immediately.

When you must confront an abuser, you can describe a scenario of a problem in the church, incorporating details of abuse that are just different enough from the abuser's actions that he will not recognize himself.[236] Allow him to pronounce judgment on the abuser. Then turn the mirror. "You are the man."

You will not be rendering injustice to the perpetrator as you begin to call him to account for his evil. When the mirror is turned to show himself, an abuser may well engage in self-justification and pity plays, but a truly repentant man, like David, will not.

Sadly, repentant abusers are incredibly rare.

Executing church discipline

By the authority of Jesus Christ, His church is to confront sin and insist on repentance. If repentance is not forthcoming, the unrepentant one is to be put out of the church (excommunicated). According to I Corinthians 5, the church should declare that, by choosing to live in

---

[234] Psalm 72:11-14.
[235] II Samuel 12.
[236] Possibly drawn from descriptions and first-person accounts in this book.

disobedience, this person cannot be in the body of Christ and must be delivered over to Satan. No Christians should engage in "Christian fellowship" with him, but should admonish him to seek the Lord.[237] This action is not so much punitive as it is to protect Christ's flock and work repentance in the offender.[238]

The Matthew 18 process of church discipline is used to deal with what we might call civil matters rather than criminal offenses, but even this process will lead to excommunication in cases in which there is no repentance.

Titus 3:10 says, "As for a person who stirs up division"—which abusers often are—"after warning him once and then twice, have nothing more to do with him." Are our churches doing that?

Several Scriptures besides these speak to the matter of church discipline. Because not all sins and not all sinners are the same, neither is the form of discipline that is applied. Some sinners are more devious and dangerous than others. Some sins are more odious to the Lord than others. For example, in I Corinthians 5, the openly defiant, shameless man was to be simply put out of the church at the very next church gathering. In some cases of serious abuse, immediate exclusion from the church is the proper means of discipline.[239] In other cases, church leaders may decide to confront the abuser and see how he responds.

If there is a display of repentance, the abuser should not be immediately welcomed back into the home of his victim. As John the Baptist said to the Pharisees, "You brood of vipers! Who warned you to

---

[237] I Corinthians 5:11 says, "But now I am writing to you not to associate with anyone who bears the name of brother if he is guilty of sexual immorality or greed, or is an idolater, reviler, drunkard, or swindler—not even to eat with such a one."

[238] For example, the prodigal son came to his senses in a pig pen. This story is told in Luke 15:11-32.

[239] Of course, making a police report is not to be neglected. Also, in cases of sexual abuse, the reality is that the perpetrator and very often his family as well *cannot* continue in your church. If a victim separates from a domestic abuser, he will also need to leave your church so that she can worship there in safety. Any other church he attends should be fully informed about who he is and what he has done.

flee from the wrath to come? Bear fruit in keeping with repentance."[240] Bearing the fruit of repentance takes time.

The sin of abuse is shameful and outrageous, an evil that should not be present among us. For the glory of Christ's name, we must faithfully apply His discipline to it.

Even though the abuser, and possibly the church, has demanded that the abuse stay private, abuse should never be considered a private matter. The light of truth needs to shine.

Thoughts from an abuse survivor

This one might not make sense until you know a little background. I read Leslie Vernick's book[241] about five months after I moved out. I tried her approach in dealing with abusive men by asking my husband what kind of husband and father he would like to be. At first he said, "I don't know," but later he told me he wanted to be the husband that held his wife's hand when they were old. At that point, I couldn't imagine getting old with him without the cycle of controlling behavior and fearful response I finally admitted we were in. This poem was written about that time.

Those Little Old Couples
That little old man
Holding hands
With that little old lady
As they walk
Gave up
The right to be right
All the time

And that little old woman
Holding his hand
Looks straight into his eyes

---

[240] Mathew 3:7-8.
[241] Vernick, *The Emotionally Destructive Marriage.*

Speaks the truth
Unafraid
Trusts the little old man
Won't make her pay
Because her little old man
Doesn't do that

And if the little old man
Hurts the little old woman
And she says stop
He already stopped
Cause he knew
He was hurting them both

He says I'm so sorry
She says I forgive you
Because she already did
That's why
They hold hands
And walk along
Like nothing is wrong
Cause it's not

It's not magic
It's not secret
It's open
And honest
Just trusting
Giving
And receiving
Love
   ~Elise Delarosa (used by permission)

A person who truly repents, turning to God and allowing God to truly transform him as a new creation in Christ, who brings forth fruit in keeping with repentance—that person can be one who holds his wife's hand when they are old.

CHAPTER 9

Taking the Role of the Good Samaritan

A high calling

If you will undertake the high calling of working for the Lord in the area of domestic abuse, not only will the abuser need to be exposed, but the victim will need to be helped. This help is not a once-and-done affair. It's a long-term commitment.

The Lord may use you to help a victim take the first step from imprisonment to freedom, by helping her begin to see her abuse for what it is. God may also call you to walk with her as she regains a normal life.

Stopping for the one

In the Biblical story of the Good Samaritan, a Jewish victim was robbed and beaten by wicked men.[242] The two religious leaders, the priest and Levite, passed by the victim, wanting to keep even their robes from touching him lest they be made unclean.

Sadly, these two represent many of our church leaders today. It was the Samaritan—the one who had most likely been taught from childhood to avoid the Jews—who stopped to help. He didn't say, "Well, you got

---

[242] Luke 10:25-37.

what you deserved. I don't have time for you." Instead, he immediately showed compassion, helped the wounded Jew with his obvious needs, took him to a place where more of his needs could be met, and paid for that meeting of those needs. Isn't this what Christianity is supposed to look like?

The priest and Levite felt contempt not only for the victim on the road, but also for Samaritans. In this story we can only imagine how their contempt must have increased, thinking that one despised person would help another despised person. But in the eyes of Jesus Christ—the one whose opinion matters—we know who did the right thing. It should be excruciatingly obvious.

> *When victim after victim asked me "Why do you care?" at first I didn't even know how to respond. I had just thought this was Christianity.*

Are *you* willing? Are you willing to stop on your busy journey on the way to somewhere and help the one who is lying bleeding by the side of the road?

Validating her efforts to resist abuse

Some who observe an abuse victim's behavior may see it as unstable or even self-defeating, but many people, even including many victims, don't realize how much victims resist abuse. Even covert resistance to the abuse is still resistance.[243] She will seek to maintain personal integrity, even if it is only within the privacy of her own mind and conscience.

If the victim tells you that she has to consider her abuser's response to anything you might suggest in her life, understand that she is simply trying to survive his irrational and cruel behavior. If she excuses behavior of his that to you seems inexcusable, the rational reason behind it may include her legitimate fear. There may be other reasons for staying in an abusive situation that the victim is too ashamed to speak about no matter how close a friend or family member you are. For

---

[243] Calgary Women's Emergency Shelter, "Honoring Resistance: How Women Resist Abuse in Intimate Relationships," www.calgarywomensshelter.com.

example, if the abuser has used her in pornographic videos, he may threaten to release those through social media, in order to shame her into staying under his control. For these, or for other reasons just as rational, she may resist your help.[244]

Changing her belief system

Several false reasons may also come into play in a victim's resistance to help. She may want to maintain the image of the fine, upstanding family. She may truly believe that she is the trash the abuser has told her she is. She may truly love him for the man she thought he was. She may fear that God will hate her and kill her if she leaves her abuser.

But the abuse victim will need to escape these false ways of thinking, despite the lies the abuser may be continuing to tell her. She will need to come to a new view of her situation and herself, resisting not only his abuse, but his manipulations and charm and plays for pity. She will have to learn to stand strong against him when he tells her that just one more proof of her love, just one more sacrifice, just one more flattening of herself will end the abuse and save the marriage.

> *I'm having to rethink what it means to be a helpmeet, what it means to submit. It used to mean just being passive. I was good at that. It suited my nature, it seemed safe. Being the opposite of passive, with my temperament, takes a tremendous amount of energy, but the more I do it, the better I get at it, doing it gracefully, even allowing myself to be misunderstood at least for a little while.*

What will a pure, respectful wife do?

In chapter six I quoted Nancy Leigh DeMoss as saying, "A wife's submission to her husband, regardless of his spiritual condition, actually releases her from fear because she has entrusted herself to God, who has ultimate control of her husband and her situation."[245] But elsewhere in the same book DeMoss appears to contradict herself when she writes,

---

[244] Other rational and legitimate reasons may include fear of losing financial support or fear of being ostracized by family and friends.

[245] DeMoss, *Lies Women Believe*, p 150.

"There are extreme situations where *an obedient wife* may need to remove herself and/or her children from proximity to her husband, if to remain in that setting would be to place themselves in *physical danger.*"[246]

But does a pure and respectful wife wait to remove herself and her children until the danger is to their bodies only?

A pure, respectful wife might show her pure, respectful behavior by resisting her abuser's impure, disrespectful, dishonest, or even criminal behavior. A pure, respectful wife might escape a situation where she will be abused, thus decreasing her abuser's opportunities to sin. A pure, respectful wife might report her husband's abusive action to law enforcement in order to help them in their God ordained task of restraining sin.[247]

> *God called me to take a step of obedience in protecting my daughters from an abusive situation at home. It was the most terrifying thing I've ever done, but I knew I had to do it.*

Be willing to go outside the camp

If there is an abuser in your church whose victim comes to you for rescue, you have been given a high calling: the calling of standing with the weak and oppressed against the powerful and winsome.

There will be a price to pay for taking up the victim's cause, and it may be high. You may have to stand against influential church people and family members who are determined to side with the abuser against the victim and anyone who stands with her. People may turn against you, and the church may be divided.

Could this be why many who see the victim choose to pass her by? Do they believe that it is less costly to them to ignore her than defend her? Perhaps in the short run it is—after all, we're busy with our own lives. But when we stand before Christ, what will *He* ask? What will *He* say?

---

[246] Ibid., p 149. Italics added.

[247] Romans 13 makes this responsibility of government very clear.

Caring for the oppressed is what our King has called us to do. He calls us to go outside the camp and bear the disgrace that he bore.[248] Perhaps some of today's churches need to be divided so that those who are anathema can be cast out and His church kept holy.[249]

No matter how much of a Christian someone may seem to be, if he or she isn't interested in pursuing mercy and truth for the weak and oppressed, this is a strong indication that he does not belong to Christ. If you turn away as the priest and Levite did, then you may well hear Christ say to you on the Last Day, "Depart from Me; I never knew you."

Be willing to be there for the long haul

Showing mercy involves more than a quick fix. Will you listen to her and believe her and take her side? Will you expose abuse for what it really is and assure her of God's justice? Will you help her with your time and money? Will you help her get to a safe place?

Typically abusers will have resources of money, influence, career, health, and position in church and society. The victim will usually lack most or all of these resources.

Helping the weak, oppressed, poor, and needy isn't popular, and it isn't glamorous. It is accomplished out of the spotlight and without encouragement from most others who claim to be Christians. The victim herself may to your surprise sometimes turn on you. But it is the right thing to do. It is love. And God is love.

> The decision to leave my spouse of thirty years was difficult, especially since he was the pastor of our church. I would often find it so hard to sit in church listening to him preach when I knew that he had been physically abusive to me and occasionally even our children and was also hiding an addiction to alcohol. I knew he was not meeting the Scriptural qualifications for an elder. I would pray, "God, how long will you let this go on. Why don't you do something? Why doesn't lightning strike him from heaven?" At some point I had asked my husband, "When should a wife, instead of submitting, act as a Christian sister by confronting her husband's sin and bringing another Christian to confront her husband

---

[248] Hebrews 13:12-13.
[249] I John 2:19; I Corinthians 11:18-19.

when he has not repented?" He said I should always act as his wife [i.e., submit].

Then I heard a song by Matthew West called "Do Something." This song is really talking about helping the poor, but every time I heard it playing in my car I cried. One Sunday sitting in church, God seemed to be saying to me, "You can do something. You can stop this."

Not long after, there was another incident involving my husband and the adult children still living at home. I knew I could not keep turning a blind eye to the damage this was doing in our home and to our children. The police asked him to leave the home, and in the morning I called an elder at our church. I knew that there would be a good chance that making that phone call would ultimately result in him losing his job and me losing my financial security, but I knew it was the right thing to do.

Praise God that the elders listened and acted to protect me and the children. Even though they tried to take steps to eventually return him to ministry, he failed to cooperate and was terminated. Eventually I filed a protective order and he filed for divorce.

I am so thankful now for a life free from abuse and the amazing peace and calm in our home. I am also thankful for God's provision through a new job that I enjoy and that meets our needs.

Showing mercy

How do you help an abuse victim in a way that is like Christ?

Listen to her

As my emotions begin to thaw, little streams of grief begin to flow. They are collecting in the basin of my soul. The water is not deep right now, just a layer of wet, but as the thaw strengthens, I fear that I may not be able to swim.

Are you willing listen to her story with compassion, and listen again and yet again as she tries to make sense of what has happened to her and tells you new pieces to add to the puzzle? Are you willing to be uncomfortable as you listen, realizing that what you hear may take you far, far outside of what you thought was possible in the realm of the church? Are you willing to listen without giving pat answers or platitudes?

Understand abuse well enough to be able to believe her

Most domestic abuse victims, by the time they come to us at our blog, A Cry for Justice, have been ignored by one church leader after another. I make it clear that I understand abuse, how an abuser thinks and acts. This means that I'll be able to tell whether or not someone making an accusation is telling the truth. And I add, "If your description matches with what I know, then no matter what high position your abuser holds or what kind of mask he wears, I'll believe you."[250]

When abuse victims learn this, they express great relief, and even astonishment. Just the fact that they will be believed is immeasurably helpful. All pastors would do well to embrace an attitude of becoming educated in abuse and taking a public stand for victims.

Expose abuse for what it is

Some victims may already understand what is happening to them. Others will know only that something is desperately wrong, and they may well even think that they are the problem. Because you are armed with knowledge and understanding of an abuser's mentality and tactics, you can confidently say,

"What you're describing is abuse. This man has regard for no one but himself. He feels entitled to control others without any sense of shame or empathy. This is not your fault, but getting educated about abuse will help you face it and deal with it."

Books and other resources that you can recommend to the victim are given on our blog, www.cryingoutforjustice.com. You can also

---

[250] Once you become familiar with the mentality and tactics of abuse as described in this book, you can recognize it when you hear it described. You'll be able to tell when someone is trying to use the accusation of abuse as an excuse to simply do what she wants. Of the many who have told me their story, I have doubted only two, because they were very focused on themselves, even more than on their own children. These allegations did later prove to be false.

encourage her to speak with professionals at the local domestic violence shelter who can help her understand that abuse isn't limited to black eyes and broken ribs.

Understanding that what she has been experiencing is actually abuse will lend a new sense of stability to the victim's thinking. Understanding her abuser's mentality and methods will help her feel a new sense of empowerment against him. When she realizes that the problem is with him rather than her and can say, "That's minimizing, that's gaslighting, that's rewriting history," she can begin to regain a firmer grounding in reality. As she begins to understand the effects that his abuse is having on her and her children, she will begin to be able to make better choices for her future.

Take her side

The confidence engendered by understanding the mentality and tactics of abuse is imperative in dealing with the abuser and in counseling the victim. Once you recognize those signs, *you can confidently side with the victim.*

Most Christian marriage counselors believe that all marriage problems should be approached as "two sinners in conflict," always using the method of couple's counseling with the goal of reconciliation, with the counselor pointing out the sin in both parties, because both are seen to be at fault. "Even if he is ninety-eight percent at fault and you are only two percent at fault, you should repent and confess of your two percent. Now try harder."

When abusive marriages are dealt with this way, it leads to disaster. The abuser gloats that he is getting away with his abuse, that he was right all along, that he bears no more guilt and blame than she does. He may even succeed in getting the counselor to believe that he is the real victim being put upon by a defective spouse.

Church counselors need to understand that in cases of abuse, one is guilty and one is innocent. One is right, and one is wrong. If the counselor fails to recognize the mentality and tactics of abuse, he will do far more harm than good.

After understanding the mentality and tactics of abusers, would you say that there is anything a victim could do to change her "two percent" that would relieve the abusive situation? Could she submit more, keep the children quieter and more obedient, mother him, keep the house more perfect, lose twenty pounds, be more seductive, cater to his every whim, console him in his tirades, and never mention her needs or desires or thoughts at all? Would that make him stop abusing and become kind and loving?

No. The root of abuse is not in the behavior of the victim but in the mentality of the abuser.

If you remain neutral in cases of abuse, you are in effect siding with the abuser. As Dietrich Bonhoeffer said, "Silence in the face of evil is itself evil: God will not hold us guiltless. Not to speak is to speak. Not to act is to act."

Don't be afraid to take sides. You *must* take a side! Take the side of righteousness. Take the side of justice. Take the side that Christ would take. Stand with the victim.

> *"All the perpetrator asks is that the bystander do nothing. He appeals to the universal desire to see, hear, and speak no evil. The victim, on the contrary, asks the bystander to share the burden of pain, the victim demands action, engagement, and remembering."*[251]

For years and sometimes decades, the abuse victim has been told "It's your fault," so much that in her confused state, she may have come to believe it. Often Christians have reinforced this attitude. If you want to overcome this way of thinking, you need to continue to repeat the truth that the abuser bears all the blame for the trouble in the relationship, and that she is not at fault. Allow none of your words to her to reflect any contrary message.

---

[251] Herman, *Trauma and Recovery*, pp 7-8.

Emphasize the justice of God

The abuse victim wants and needs rescue and justice and vindication. If in her confused mind she continues to think of herself as worthless trash, it's important to help her understand toxic shame and to remind her of God's love.

At this point, it isn't necessary to mention forgiveness, and certainly not reconciliation. When I faced a case of sexual abuse in 2008 at the church I pastor, I wrongly pressed the father of the victim to immediately forgive the perpetrator, even preaching about mercy and forgiveness. Eventually, though, the father did forgive—he forgave me for my ignorance and arrogance.

Unequivocally, the abuse victim needs to hear that God hates the evil that has been perpetrated against her. Reading an imprecatory Psalm may well be appropriate.[252] She needs to hear that God is ready to rise up and deliver her. She needs to hear that God will strike down the evil ones who enslave others. She needs to hear Christians saying, "We will love you with the love of Christ. We will protect and shield you. This evil angers God, and it angers us too. We will stand with you against the evil and against the one who is perpetrating it."

Don't take over her life

Victims of abuse have long been told by their abuser what to think and what to do.[253] As a result, they might have problems thinking for themselves and making decisions.

It is important for those who want to offer genuine help to be different from the abuser. We need to help her to think, but not tell her what to think. Instead of giving commands or advice, we can make suggestions and ask questions. Instead of "You need to leave him right now," we can ask questions like "Have you considered leaving him? Why do you think leaving might be a good idea? What happened when you tried to leave him before?" This can help her to think through the matter

---

[252] Imprecatory psalms are ones in which David calls on God to judge the wicked. Some of them are Psalms 5, 10, 17, 35, 58, 59, 69, 70, 79, 83, 109, 129, 137, and 140.

[253] Bancroft, *Why Does He Do That?* Location 260, Kindle edition.

for herself, something she has not been given the chance to do by her abuser.[254]

We can provide help and information, we can listen and help them sort out their thoughts, but we must leave the final decisions to the abuse victims themselves. They need to be able to learn by making their own decisions, even if some of their decisions may be wrong.

> *Sara treated me with respect, even though my choice to see Joe again was such a poor one. Never once did Sara say "I told you so" or imply that she thought badly of me. I could tell she didn't think badly of me as a person, even though she had known all along that my choice to see Joe again was a dangerous one. Because Sara was able to be my anchor, I was able to get through a terrifying and embarrassing time of my life with my self-esteem intact.*[255]

Expect trouble

When Sanballat came against Nehemiah, pretending to want to simply meet with him, but insidiously designing to derail the work of building the walls of Jerusalem, Nehemiah refused to interact with him at all.[256] He understood that Sanballat had nefarious designs and didn't seem bothered by the thought that he might have a legitimate complaint. When we stand with the victim against her enemy, we can also expect insidious attacks. The abuser may threaten. He may want to meet with us to "talk."

If pastors feel that they need to listen to every Sanballat who comes along, believing the false notions that all sins are equal and every accusation holds a germ of truth, the Lord's true work will surely be hindered. Perhaps the ones bringing the charges are actually of the enemy, with the goal of subverting the work of God and destroying the walls of His church. So it is in the case of the abuser.

---

[254] *Helping Her Get Free: A Guide for Families and Friends of Abused Women,* by MSSW Susan Brewster (Seal Press, 2006), offers excellent counsel for those who are trying to help friends or family members escape abusers and stay safe.

[255] Brewster, *Helping Her Get Free,* pp 94-95.

[256] This story is told in Nehemiah 6.

182 • CHAPTER 9

Meeting her needs

Safety

If she fears for her safety, then she is probably not safe. Don't assume that because her abuser is a church member her fears are irrational; if she fears for her life, take her seriously. She surely knows better than you do that "nice guys" can kill their wives and children.

> *We never could tell what word or even a look from one of us might set him off into a home-destroying rage. This tyranny of shouting and smashing and hurting could go on all evening, or even break out in the middle of the night when we might find ourselves being jerked out of bed. Even the family pet wasn't safe. Sometimes we would sneak out of the house and find a place to hide for hours.*[257]

Some questions you can ask to help assess the risk of abuse would include these: Has the abuse been increasing in intensity? Has he sexually abused her? Has he been violent in the past, or made threats against the victim, the children, other family members, or the family's animals? Does the abuser have guns or other weapons? Has he abused drugs or alcohol? Is he mentally unstable? Has he threatened suicide?

The degree of the victim's isolation is another factor to consider in evaluating her safety level. Also, abuse often escalates when she is pregnant or has just given birth. Another of the most dangerous periods is during her plan to escape and in the days and weeks shortly after her escape.[258]

If you feel that you are in over your head in helping your friend, especially in regard to her physical safety, talk to the police or the local women's shelter for advice.[259] They can help with accessing many

---

[257] Crippen and Wood, *A Cry for Justice*, p 76.

[258] See the section in this chapter called "Helping after separation" for more information on this problem.

[259] Safety planning for abuse victims is a subject of its own. Many women's resource centers provide training in this important area, equipping people to recognize red flags that signal high-risk abuse. Pastors and church members would do well to obtain such training. Also see "How to assess the risk a victim is facing," http://notunderbondage.com/pages/how-to-assess-the-risk-a-victim-is-facing-1

resources such as victim-protection programs, address-protection programs, even possibly changing her social security number. They can also provide safe housing for a victim who fears for her safety.

Finances

Because abusers keep their victims poor in order to control them, you may find when you help a victim that she has very few assets. Christians without understanding will often think, "Well, no wonder she's struggling financially. She's the one who decided to leave him. She made her bed, and now she's lying in it."

We should be ashamed to think this way. We should be the first ones to leap to fulfill the needs of the broken, the despised, the outcast, the oppressed. Will we be as guilty as the abuser in having no empathy for the abused? Can we put ourselves in the same situation and see ourselves escaping with our souls barely intact? Can we imagine the position we would be in? And we dare not say, "But this would never happen to me."

When the victim has been able to escape her abuser, financial difficulties rarely abate. She may need help finding a job or renewing long-dormant job skills or developing new ones. The abuser will commonly resist paying child support because he can't stand the thought of giving money to a victim who is no longer under his direct control. He will often return to court multiple times to try to get the payments reduced.

Medical and legal needs

A wide range of physical ailments such as those described in Chapter 5 are also common in domestic abuse survivors, and understanding friends and supporters will go far in helping her as she tries to find ways to deal with these issues.

Victims will also need attorneys who are truly aware of the dynamics of abuse. (Unfortunately, these attorneys are not as common as they should be.) Victims will need friends and other supporters who will be willing to stand by them when they have to face their abuser in court— we've heard of many stories of the abusers sitting with their side full of church supporters, while the victim sits alone. This should never be.

Mental health needs

It shouldn't be surprising if an abuse victim has developed some form of mental or emotional instability because of all the trauma that has been inflicted. This is *not* to say that she is crazy. But long-term abuse does leave deep emotional and mental scars, often manifestations of post-traumatic stress disorder, as was discussed in Chapter 5.

You can encourage her that there is no shame in visiting a mental health professional or other professional or even, if necessary, getting on medication to help stabilize her emotional state.

Help with troubled children

Outsiders may look askance at the family life of the domestic abuse victim who has left her abuser, thinking that she simply can't keep her children under control. Those who have never experienced domestic abuse will find it difficult to understand the pressure and trauma experienced by the children, which, when the pressure is released, can come out in a myriad of ways. Often the victim has also learned to leave discipline to the abuser or to discipline in a way that satisfies him, so that when he is no longer in the picture she may find herself in the position of needing to learn—or relearn—how to best lead her family.

Empathy and patience will play large parts in your understanding walk and refusal to categorize the victim as a "bad parent."

Help in relating anew to God and others

For many victims of domestic abuse, every single relationship has been affected. The person that the victim thought she loved and trusted has abused her. She doubts the wisdom and goodness of God. Her children have heard her mocked and belittled in their presence. In many cases she and the children have been told that her parents and friends are untrustworthy.

The victim will need to walk the road of learning to trust God and His people again. Depending on how severe her abuse has been, she may need to be reminded again and again that God is trustworthy and that some of those who claim His Name are trustworthy. As true followers of Christ walk with her on her journey of recovery from abuse, their love will be the best representation of the love of God she can see. As a victim heals from the abusive relationship, it is vital for her to establish these healthy relationships with others.

Victims also need to be counseled as to how to avoid abusive relationships in the future. Though there are a number of books that address this issue, *The Gift of Fear* by Gavin De Becker is especially helpful.[260]

Of the victims I have had the privilege to correspond with and meet, the strongest are those who have a living relationship with Christ. I'll talk more about that in the last chapter of this book.

Helping after the escape

The most dangerous time in the life of a victim is the few weeks or months before and after her escape. Women who have left their abusers or are in the process of leaving are in serious danger of being injured or killed.[261] In addition to the need for physical safety after escape, the abuse survivor will need help from other new kinds of attacks.

Abuse through stalking

When one person pursues another person for a period of time in such a way that it poses a threat to the one being pursued, causing reasonable fear, this is stalking.[262] Stalking can be carried out through the overt means that we would associate with the act, such as actually following the victim and showing up where she happens to be or driving near her home or leaving notes on her car. It can also be

---

[260] Gavin de Becker, *The Gift of Fear and Other Survival Signals that Protect Us from Violence* (Dell, 1998). One section of the book is devoted exclusively to domestic abuse.

[261] "About one-fifth of the female IPH [intimate partner homicide] victims who had a restraining order were killed within two days of the order being issued; about one-third were killed within a month." See http://injuryprevention.bmj.com/content/14/3/191.abstract.

[262] J. Reid Meloy, ed., *The Psychology of Stalking: Clinical and Forensic Perspectives* (Academic Press of San Diego, 1998).

undertaken through technological contacts such as phone calls, texts, emails, and social media connections.

Stalking can move to a new level when the stalker spies on the victim or her friends or family members, either in person or through technology. The stalker can secretly enter the victim's home and leave a subtle sign that he has been there. He can deliver unwanted gifts or leave messages in cryptic language or code that the victim will understand to be threatening but that the abuser can deny to mean any kind of threat.

For us to truly help an abuse victim who is experiencing this kind of threat hanging over her life, we will have to not only understand the significance of the threat imposed by stalking, but continue to let the abuser know that his victim is no longer alone and is being supported.

Abuse in spite of the restraining order

If a victim fears her abuser after separation, she will have to make the decision as to whether or not to get a restraining order, or order of protection, which means that it would be illegal for the abuser to come within a certain distance of her or the children. However, though obtaining a restraining order may sound attractive, there are reasons to hesitate. An abuser bent on destruction will not be stopped by a piece of paper and a threat of jail time. Sometimes the restraining order itself can even cause the abuser's rage to increase.[263] This is a decision that should be made with prayerful wisdom and the advice of wise counselors who understand abuse.

Abuse through custody battles

After separation, since the abuser often can't get to his victim directly, one of the ways he can abuse is through the children, especially in court through custody battles. Make no mistake, the abuser fights for custody not because he loves and values his children. If that were the case, he wouldn't have abused them and his primary victim in the first place. Rather, he has objectified the children as his property, just as he

---

[263] Gavin de Becker, *The Gift of Fear*, pp 223-224.

has objectified his primary victim. In his mind they are his chattel that he is entitled to possess and control.

The abuser will also pursue custody as a means to exercise his power and control against his victim while looking good to those on the outside, as one who really loves his children. Each court battle is also a new opportunity to publicly shame his victim, effectively putting her on trial for each new frivolous charge. He will point to her mental health struggles that *he* caused as a reason she is unfit to keep the children. He will point to the children's misbehaviors, which resulted from *his* abuse, as a reason she is unfit to keep them.

If the children do not want to see the abuser, then the abuser and his allies will often claim that the victim has turned the children against him. In court his lawyer will cite "parental alienation."[264]

> *The abuser's lawyer brought an "expert witness" into the courtroom, who said he could tell that the children had been brainwashed by looking at their eyes from across the room. Fortunately, the sensible judge threw out that "expert" testimony.*

Because abusers often represent themselves in court, they can pursue custody and other litigation for years without great cost to themselves.[265] The victim, on the other hand, faces burdensome legal fees in addition to the fear looming with each new letter from the abuser's lawyer, each new accusation, each new court date. In addition to the other issues she faces such as physical and emotional issues for both herself and her children, the increased financial pressure and anxiety from the constant legal actions can push her to despair.

Each time she enters the courtroom doors, she does it with the awareness that her children may be forced to spend more time with an

---

[264] Though the general way of thinking in our society is that all children will want to spend time with both parents, this idea doesn't even make sense in the context of abuse. Anyone involved in a custody case who understand abuse—and sadly, these individuals are rare—will know that it is only logical that children who have lived through abuse will not want to see their abuser.

[265] I have personally witnessed an abuser who was acting as his own attorney cross examine his victim in court. This emphasizes how important it is for us to support an abuse survivor long after she has left her abuser.

abuser who is continuing to abuse. She may wonder, because of her most recent struggle in some other area of her life, if this time her children may be taken away from her altogether. How can she endure?

I can't possibly overstate the importance of members of the body of Christ being willing to walk with the victim every single time she has to enter those courtroom doors.

Abuse through visitation

The idea that children are always better off having a relationship with both parents is a fallacy, but courts rarely see it that way. Imagine being a parent whose children have been sexually molested or physically beaten by the abuser. Because she can't prove the abuse in court, she has to live with the abuser's triumph in being able to play the system to gain partial custody or at least visitation. She would like to be able to move far away from the abuser, but she will often find herself bound by court-ordered visitation to have to stay in the same area.

There are a number of ways that an abuser will seek to continue to abuse his victim through the children, whose welfare he sees as inconsequential in the battle. He may elicit details about the victim's life from the children, thus effectively using them as spies. He may use the children to deliver veiled threats or orders to his victim. He may seek to confuse them with lies and manipulate their emotions to feel pity for him. He may even reveal private details about his victim to the children in order to shame her.

Imagine being a child in this situation. Though court-ordered visitation with an abuser is preferable to living with the abuser full time, still it is a serious hindrance to the peace and stability children need for recovery. Each time between visits, the child can calm down and begin to experience stability and safety. Emotional and physical symptoms will begin to improve. Then after just a weekend court-ordered visit with the abuser, the child will regress again, losing sleep, withdrawing or acting out, and sometimes having to miss school.

Periods of calm interrupted by periods of manipulation and control can keep the child on a perpetual roller coaster. Of course, whatever turmoil the child experiences, the custodial parent will experience as well.

Don't give up

If you undertake to help a domestic abuse victim, some people in the churches might even see you as an enemy of the cause of Christ. But God may call you to educate your church about this important matter, because He is bringing the hidden things to light.

Once again, the need for wise, loving friends in abusive situations as well as other caring, supportive Christians is just as great as the need for wise counselors. There is much for the people of God to do.

> To the choirmaster. A psalm of David. A song.
> God shall arise, his enemies shall be scattered;
>   and those who hate him shall flee before him!
> As smoke is driven away, so you shall drive them away;
>   as wax melts before fire, so the wicked shall perish before God!
> But the righteous shall be glad; they shall exult before God;
>   they shall be jubilant with joy!
> Sing to God, sing praises to his name;
>   lift up a song to him who rides through the deserts;
> His name is the LORD; exult before him!
> Father of the fatherless and protector of widows
>   is God in his holy habitation.
> God settles the solitary in a home;
> He leads out the prisoners to prosperity,
>   but the rebellious dwell in a parched land.[266]

---

[266] Psalm 68:1-6.

CHAPTER 10

The Written Word and the Living Word

When I began speaking on the topic of domestic abuse, I did something radical. I knew that the evangelical church was grossly ignorant about the mentality and tactics of abuse, resulting in great injustice. Because of this, I advised my listeners to read books I recommended, some of which were written by professionals who didn't claim Christianity, in order to become wise about these issues. When I did this, someone told me I would be accused of denying the sufficiency of Scripture.

But is it true that the Bible claims to be the only source needed to counsel anyone in any situation? Is it true that if we recommend anything else we're going against God?

The written Word is not sufficient for all understanding

The Bible is sufficient "for faith and life"

The Word of God was written by men who were inspired by the Holy Spirit. The 1689 London Confession of Faith[267] states, "The Holy Scripture is the only sufficient, certain, and infallible rule of all saving

---

[267] One of several such confessions of faith making a similar statement.

knowledge, faith, and obedience," and the Bible contains "all things necessary for [God's] own glory, man's salvation, faith, and life."

As T. David Gordon explains, "'faith and life' are shorthands for the *beliefs* of the covenant community and the *duties* of the covenant community."[268]

The second half of the 1689 London Confession of Faith statement furthermore declares,

> Nevertheless, we acknowledge the inward illumination of the Spirit of God to be necessary for the saving understanding of such things as are revealed in the Word, and that there are some circumstances concerning the worship of God, and government of the church, common to human actions and societies, *which are to be ordered by the light of nature and Christian prudence, according to the general rules of the Word, which are always to be observed.*[269]

Notice that the men who wrote the 1689 London Confession of Faith believed that there are some circumstances "common to human actions and societies," that are to be understood "by the light of nature and Christian prudence." Though they are to be applied in a way that would be consistent with Scripture, they are not addressed in Scripture directly or even indirectly. T. David Gordon writes,

> The Bible is sufficient to guide the human-as-covenanter [the Christian] but *not* sufficient to guide the human-as-mechanic, the human-as-physician, the human-as-businessman, the human-as-parent, the human-as-husband, the human-as-wife, or the human-as-legislator. . . .[270]

John Frame, in *The Doctrine of the Christian Life,* says, "[S]ufficiency in the present context is *not sufficiency of specific information* but sufficiency

---

[268] T. David Gordon, "The Insufficiency of Scripture," *Modern Reformaton* (January/February 2002), pp 18-23. Italics added.

[269] 1689 London Confession of Faith. Italics added.

[270] Gordon, "The Insufficiency of Scripture."

of divine words. Scripture contains divine words sufficient for all of life."[271]

God also instructs through observation

John Frame goes on to say,

> People sometimes misunderstand the doctrine of sufficiency by thinking that it excludes the use of any extra-biblical information in reaching ethical conclusions. But if we exclude the use of extra-biblical information, then ethical reflection is next to impossible.
>
> Scripture itself recognizes this point. As I said earlier, the inscriptional curses do not forbid seeking extra-biblical information. Rather, they forbid us to equate extra-biblical information with divine words.
>
> The same is true for all divine commands in Scripture. When God tells Israel to honor fathers and mothers, he does not bother to . . . set forth an exhaustive list of things that may honor or dishonor them. Rather, God assumed that Israel have some general knowledge of family life, and he expects them to apply his commands to that knowledge. [272]

T. David Gordon observes,

> Wisdom does not come easily or quickly, but through a lengthy, prolonged effort. Most importantly, it does not come exclusively, or perhaps even primarily, through Bible study. Solomon promotes listening to parents, elders, a variety of counselors, and even a consideration of ants, badgers, locusts, and lizards.[273]

Through the illuminating power of the Holy Spirit, the Scriptures show us the need for Jesus Christ, show us how to come to Christ, show us Jesus Christ Himself, and show us what life in Christ looks like. But

---

[271] John Frame, *The Doctrine of the Christian Life* (P&R Publishing, 2008), p 157. Italics added.
[272] Ibid, p 163.
[273] Gordon, "The Insufficiency of Scripture."

for us to believe that the Bible contains "all things necessary for . . . life"[274] does not mean we need never go outside the Bible to learn anything about this life. God has not spoken to us exhaustively in the Bible about all things pertaining to this life. Many important things can be learned from natural revelation.

In my own situation, our church experienced a case of severe sexual abuse. Because of that, I began studying books about the issue to learn warning signs of predators and protect our people, none of which is spelled out in the Scriptures.[275]

God also instructs through experience

Though the Bible is sufficient to provide all the knowledge we need for our understanding about saving faith and obedience, the more mature we become in Christ, the better we will understand the nature of the things that Scripture explains. In order to be fully competent in counseling others in a given experience, we must be trained in the school of experience ourselves.

Second Corinthians 1:3-5 says that as God comforts us in our trials, we will be able to comfort others. But how can we understand what is meant by this Scripture unless we actually experience the comfort? And how can we experience the comfort unless we have experienced a trial?

I may study the Bible for years and thoroughly and accurately learn all of its doctrines. But in order to connect the truth of Scripture to life, as it is illuminated by the Holy Spirit to show us Christ in the midst of the trial, I must have experience of a trial.

However, many counselors who have never had any experience in the world in which the abuse victim lives have nevertheless taken their own paradigm and applied it to the victim's situation.

The place of psychology in life instruction

The Holy Scriptures certainly teach us about sin and its tactics, about the mentality and methods of abuse, but neither exhaustively nor in

---

[274] 1689 London Confession of Faith.

[275] I quickly began to see that the people who wrote from a secular perspective knew far more about the subject than those who wrote from a Christian perspective. This should not be.

completely fleshed out detail. The science of how the human mind works is not to be ignored or minimized by Christians. To ignore it—to somehow think of it as unholy and unnecessary—is to cut oneself off from wisdom. Christians have been afraid of the study of the human mind and behavior, but without foundation.[276]

We have been ignorant and arrogant. As a result, we exacerbate the plight of abuse victims.

Psychology is defined as "the scientific study of the nature, functioning, and development of the human mind, including the faculties of reason, emotion, perception, communication, etc. . . . based on observation of the behavior of individuals or groups of individuals in particular . . . circumstances."[277] Psychology in its most basic form is simply one type of wise observation.[278]

As Clinton McLemore says, psychology can serve as one of the tools to help us understand how human beings think and interact with one another. Our job as Christians is to interpret that data in light of the Word of God and its teachings about sin, conscience, man's alienation from God, and the truth of real salvation. If we do this, then the information we have gained can be truly helpful.[279]

---

[276] The branch of Christian counseling formerly known as nouthetic counseling, developed in 1972 by Jay Adams, claims to eschew psychology. However, one of the most basic tenets of the nouthetic counseling model is the development of certain habits in the life of the counselee. In 1961 psychologists Ernest R. Hilgard and Donald George Marquis wrote, "The conditioned response was called the unit of habit by psychologists, to whom habit was the most important concept in psychology." (*Conditioning and Learning*, published by Appleton-Century-Crofts, p 19). In claiming to abjure psychology, nouthetic practitioners are actually practicing a form of it.

[277] *Oxford English Dictionary* (Oxford University Press, 2013), definition of *psychology*.

[278] It is when psychologists try to find solutions to problems that they often fall short. In analyzing the problems themselves, the body of knowledge gained by psychologists can be immensely helpful.

[279] Clinton W. McLemore, *Toxic Relationships and How to Change Them* (Jossey-Bass, 2003), pp 22-23.

Born in a North Korean prison camp, Shin Dong Hyuk escaped in 2005 and eventually found asylum in the United States.[280] Every true Christian would want him to realize his need for the Savior and find his salvation in Jesus Christ.

But in order to offer wise, loving help to this refugee, a discerning Christian will make the effort to understand about the life of abuse he endured. In order to help him recover from the horrors of life in the most oppressive regime in the world—in a prison camp where people treated each other like animals—a wise Christ-follower will want to have enough empathy to listen and learn what survival conditions were like for him there, how the prison guards abused the prisoners, how the prisoners abused each other, and how all of them lived under the shadow of the master abuser, the Supreme Leader of North Korea. They will also want to understand the effects of trauma on the human body and mind that cause a person coming from the prison camps to have difficulty with trust, cause their memories to be fragmented, and cause them to continue to experience night terrors, flashbacks, and dissociation.[281]

The same is true for those who have suffered under domestic abusers with a mentality of entitlement and justification, with no shame or empathy. These problems of abuse are not described at length in the Bible, but all of them are important for us grasp in order to be able to offer true, loving help.

The study of the brain, the study of trauma, and the study of various ways that people interact with each other are legitimate branches of learning. Just as we listen to and learn about people from history, just as we learn about other parts of the human body from medical researchers, just as we learn about the way the physical world works from scientists and those in the practical professions, so Christians must listen to and

[280] Blaine Harden, *Escape from Camp 14: One Man's Remarkable Odyssey from North Korea to Freedom in the West* (Penguin, 2013). Though some details of the account have been recanted or challenged, Shin is still widely believed to be the only person born in a North Korean prison camp known to have escaped and survived.

[281] *The Body Keeps the Score: Brain, Mind, and Body in the Healing of Trauma,* by Bessel van der Kolk (Viking, 2014), is one of the best books available on the subject.

learn from those who have studied the topics related to the mentality and tactics of abusers and the effects they have on the victims. Lundy Bancroft, for example, has studied thousands of abusive men and interviewed their victims. Because the Bible is not his final authority, he will fall short in his solution for the problem of abuse, but because of his years of experience with and observation of the ways abusers think and act, he has a wealth of information available to those who will listen.[282]

When Christians reject the findings of such careful, scientific observers, they bring no glory to God. In fact, they might even appear as fools, and justifiably so.[283]

Psychological studies can help us understand more about how the human mind and soul function. But they are incapable of touching the deepest needs of the soul. Only Jesus Christ can do that.

Jesus Christ, our true Deliverer

But as for me, my prayer is to you, O LORD.
At an acceptable time, O God, in the abundance of your steadfast love
answer me in your saving faithfulness.
Deliver me from sinking in the mire;
let me be delivered from my enemies and from the deep waters.
Let not the flood sweep over me, or the deep swallow me up,
or the pit close its mouth over me.
Answer me, O LORD, for your steadfast love is good;
according to your abundant mercy, turn to me.
Hide not your face from your servant;
for I am in distress; make haste to answer me.
Draw near to my soul, redeem me;
ransom me because of my enemies!
You know my reproach, and my shame and my dishonor;
my foes are all known to you.

---

[282] *Why Does He Do That? Inside the Minds of Angry and Controlling Men* (Berkley Books, 2003).

[283] Books such as *Psychoheresy* and *The End of Christian Psychology*, both by Martin Bobgan, excoriate scientific study regarding the mind, and sometimes appear to promote the idea of a united effort in psychology to discredit everything the Bible says.

Reproaches have broken my heart,
  so that I am in despair.
I looked for pity, but there was none,
  and for comforters, but I found none.[284]

We cannot effect a complete rescue

We at A Cry for Justice regularly hear true stories from abuse victims, heart-breaking stories, describing what seem like absolutely hopeless circumstances. They elicit in us a zeal to help and rescue and deliver.

But often we, along with the victim, are at a loss as to how to effect that rescue.

How do you rescue a suffering woman with little children who is under court order to maintain visitation contact with a sociopath? How do you "fix" that?

How do you whisk a victim away into hiding, provide a house and support her and her children so that her psychopathic abuser who has vowed to kill her if she leaves him will never find her?

How do you ensure that an abuse survivor will receive justice from the family court system? How do you provide the thousands and thousands of dollars for her legal fees?

How do you convince her church, which has already dealt her injustice, that they are wrong and have been duped by the abuser?

How do you heal her from all the effects and trauma of the decades of abuse?

How? And the answer is I cannot always do these things. Even if I had billions of dollars at my disposal, these are things in many cases that I simply could not fix. (Though be assured I would certainly try!)

There have been other people down through history in what looked like totally hopeless situations.

The foremen of the people of Israel saw that they were in trouble when they said, "You shall by no means reduce your

---

[284] Psalm 69:13-20.

number of bricks, your daily task each day." They met Moses and Aaron, who were waiting for them, as they came out from Pharaoh; and they said to them, "The LORD look on you and judge, because you have made us stink in the sight of Pharaoh and his servants, and have put a sword in their hand to kill us." Then Moses turned to the LORD and said, "O LORD, why have you done evil to this people? Why did you ever send me? For since I came to Pharaoh to speak in your name, he has done evil to this people, and you have not delivered your people at all."[285]

The hammer fell. End of story?

Every victim of this evil of abuse has, I am sure, at one time or another felt or even verbalized those very words to the Lord: ". . . he has done evil to me, and You have not delivered me at all."

Through our ministry at A Cry for Justice, we are able to help many people. Primarily we help abuse victims by validating them. We believe them. We give them a forum that is safe where they can cry out and tell their stories and know that they will be believed. We help them see that they are not alone and what is happening to them has a name. But we cannot effect *exodus and deliverance.*

There is, however, One who can and does.

The only One who can fully rescue

There is one ultimate and complete revelation of God to man. He is the same one who humbled the mightiest ruler and power of Moses' day and brought His people from slavery into freedom. His name is Jesus Christ, and He is our Deliverer. In fact, that was the very purpose of His redemptive mission into this fallen world—to deliver victims of cruel abuse and oppression.

> Since therefore the children share in flesh and blood, he himself likewise partook of the same things, that through death he might destroy the one who has the power of death, that is, the

---

[285] Exodus 5:19-23.

devil, and deliver all those who through fear of death were subject to lifelong slavery.[286]

One of the most encouraging and remarkable things that I have learned over these last years in this ministry to abuse victims is how a depressingly hopeless situation can be radically changed to one of healing and hope, sometimes in a surprisingly short period of time.

One victim/survivor I have known for a number of years told me not long ago, "I don't even recognize my life now." Her history was one of treacherous abuse and oppression, filled with despair, days one after another given to feeling like just giving up. Yet today she can say:

I waited patiently for the L̲ORD*; he inclined to me and heard my cry.*

He drew me up from the pit of destruction, out of the miry bog,

and set my feet upon a rock, making my steps secure.

He put a new song in my mouth, a song of praise to our God.

Many will see and fear, and put their trust in the L̲ORD*.*

Blessed is the man who makes the L̲ORD *his trust,*

who does not turn to the proud, to those who go astray after a lie! [287]

What does Christ's rescue look like?

I do not know specifically how the Lord is going to set your feet on that rock, but I do know if you genuinely cry out to Him for deliverance and if you put your faith and trust in the Lord Jesus Christ, the Son of God, the only Redeemer and Savior from sin and evil and death and destruction, *He will hear you.*

This we know without doubt from His Word, the Bible, *Christ Jesus came into this world to save the lost and rescue the oppressed,* and that salvation includes freedom from the greatest abuser of all time, Satan.

Christ loves the humble and broken, His eye is upon the oppressed, and it is His desire that His people be set free.

---

[286] Hebrews 2:14-15.

[287] Psalm 40:1-4.

He regards the prayer of the destitute
 and does not despise their prayer.
Let this be recorded for a generation to come,
 so that a people yet to be created may praise the LORD:
that he looked down from his holy height;
 from heaven the LORD looked at the earth,
to hear the groans of the prisoners,
 to set free those who were doomed to die. . . .[288]

Let those who fear the LORD say, "His steadfast love endures forever."
Out of my distress I called on the LORD;
 the LORD answered me and set me free.
The LORD is on my side; I will not fear.
What can man do to me?
The LORD is on my side as my helper;
I shall look in triumph on those who hate me.[289]

The Bible is filled with these kinds of statements and promises. Our Creator and Rescuer desires good for us. He hates the wicked abuser, and He is *justice* in His very being.

No one knows how or when the Lord will bring you out of oppression and into freedom and peace. But I know that He never fails to hear the cries of the afflicted. In fact, He *delights* to deliver them from what look like hopeless odds.

> *The Philistine said to David, "Come to me, and I will give your flesh to the birds of the air and to the beasts of the field." Then David said to the Philistine, "You come to me with a sword and with a spear and with a javelin, but I come to you in the name of the LORD of hosts, the God of the armies of Israel, whom you have defied. This day the LORD will deliver you into my hand, and I will strike you down and cut off your head. And I will give the dead bodies of the host of the Philistines*

---

[288] Psalm 102:17-20.
[289] Psalm 118:4-7.

*this day to the birds of the air and to the wild beasts of the earth, that
all the earth may know that there is a God in Israel."*[290]

Open to the Psalms, even in the most hopeless of times in your life.
Listen to Christ speak to you there. Hear His certain promises. See how
He rescues the weak and weary. Pour out your heart to Him in all
honesty, put your trust in Him alone as your Deliverer, and keep on
crying out to Him for justice.

> *One day it hit me all at once just how cruel my husband was being to me. I
> honestly believe I had been in denial about that fact until that moment.
> Immediately, God spoke one word directly into my heart. "Enough." As in,
> "You have done everything you could think of to do, you have suffered
> enough, and you can in good conscience stop your efforts and let it be."*
>
> *At the same time, He released me from my emotional desperation to keep
> a husband who was no longer a husband to me in any way other than on
> paper. My fear was replaced by a supernatural calm. I didn't know what
> would come next, but I knew I was going to be okay.*

When the Lord tells an abuse victim "Enough," she is disobeying if
she continues to take the abuse. It may be extremely difficult. Others
may walk away or even turn against her. And yet He promises in Isaiah
43:2 to all those who keep their eyes on Him and their hearts fixed on
Him,

When you pass through the waters, I will be with you;
and through the rivers, they shall not overwhelm you;
when you walk through fire you shall not be burned,
and the flame shall not consume you.

Your church may not hear you. Your relatives may disbelieve and
abandon you. People you thought were your good friends may walk
away from you. But I can tell you with all confidence and certainly, *Jesus
Christ the Lord will never, ever abandon you.* And He promises in Romans
10:11, "Everyone who believes in him will not be put to shame."

---

[290] I Samuel 17:44-46.

The Just Judge will set things right

Jesus Christ hates evil, and He keeps his promises. He has walked through each situation and understands it. He is there. Judgment of the oppressors will come, if not fully in this life, then without fail and completely in the life to come.

In the midst of vexation and grief of hearing evil called good and good called evil—while the privileges of abusers are supported and their victims maligned—is this hope: we can know that the Just One will return and overturn it all. Those who are afflicted now will be forever comforted in the presence of perfect love.

As we work for justice and righteousness in the Name of the great Judge of all, we ask for divinely inspired wisdom, strategy, words, and power. We pray for all those fighting the battle without ceasing and join them with prayers for endurance and wisdom. We do not fight men alone but powers of darkness that seek to blot out the Light, yet cannot.

May the Lord bless you and keep you. May He make His face shine upon you and give you peace.

To the One who is the true and righteous possessor of power and control, be all glory and honor and praise forever and ever, Amen.

Your sin
The sin you could not see
The sin you will not see
Has driven me
Straight into the arms of another

He is ever so much
Stronger than you
But He doesn't punish me
When I disagree
Or when I have my own opinion
Or when I cry

He doesn't hurt me
The way you hurt me
And he never turns away
To pay me back

As the picture
Of your angry face fades away
I see His loving face
Much clearer
Echoes of your ugly words
Fade as I hear God's voice
Wisdom
Truth
Hope

I must have forgotten how to breathe
Cause I kept holding my breath
Waiting for other shoes to fall
And they did

I used to be so afraid
But now I can't quite remember
Why I was ever so afraid of you
Or why I hated who I became
Because of you

Now I'm learning to breathe
All over again
And I'm living in peace
All over again
And letting myself feel
All over again

Sometimes I cry
Just a little
But really I'm okay
It's different now
I don't sob suffering
Rocking back and forth
Holding my head
Wishing I could make it stop
Or God would make it stop
Or anyone would make it stop
Anyone at all
Especially you

I choose to trust Him Who Is
I live loving Him
And I stand knowing
I completely know
That the one who holds me closely
And will never let me go
Died and rose again
So He could pay for
Your sin
  ~Elise Delarosa (used by permission)

Selected Bibliography

Annis, Ann W., Michelle Loyd-Paige, and Rodger R. Rice. *Set us Free: What the Church Needs to Know from Survivors of Abuse.* Calvin College Social Research Center and University Press of America, 2001.

Bancroft, Lundy. *When Dad Hurts Mom: Helping Your Children Heal the Wounds of Witnessing Abuse.* Berkley Books, 2004.

---. *Why Does He Do That? Inside the Minds of Angry and Controlling Men.* Berkley Books, 2003.

Bancroft, Lundy, and Jay G. Silverman. *The Batterer as Parent: Addressing the Impact of Domestic Violence on Family Dynamics.* Sage, 2002.

Braun, Sarah, and Bridget Flynn. *Honeymoon and Hell: A Memoir of Abuse.* Sarah Braun, 2010.

Brewster, Susan, MSSW. *Helping Her Get Free: A Guide for Families and Friends of Abused Women.* Seal Press, 2006.

Cloud, Henry, and John Townsend. *Boundaries: When to Say Yes, How to Say No to Take Control of Your Life.* Zondervan, 1992.

Crippen, Jeff, and Anna Wood. *A Cry for Justice: How the Evil of Domestic Abuse Hides in Your Church!* Calvary Press, 2012.

de Becker, Gavin. *The Gift of Fear and Other Survival Signals that Protect Us from Violence.* Dell, 1997.

Evans, Patricia. *Victory over Verbal Abuse: A Healing Guide to Renewing Your Spirit and Reclaiming Your Life.* Adams Media, 2011.

Hare, Robert D. *Without Conscience: The Disturbing World of the Psychopaths Among Us.* The Guilford Press, 1999.

Herman, Judith. *Trauma and Recovery: The Aftermath of Violence—from Domestic Abuse to Political Terror.* Basic Books, 2015.

Ingraham, Dale with Rebecca Davis. *Tear Down this Wall of Silence: Dealing with Sexual Abuse in Our Churches (an introduction for those who will hear).* Ambassador International, 2015.

Instone-Brewer, David. *Divorce and Remarriage in the Church: Biblical Solutions for Pastoral Realities.* IVP Books, 2006.

Jantz, Dr. Gregory L., and Ann McMurray. *Healing the Scars of Emotional Abuse.* Revell, 2009.

Johnson, Scott Allen. *Physical Abusers and Sexual Offenders: Forensic and Clinical Strategies.* CRC Press, 2006.

Kroeger, Catherine Clark and Nancy Nason-Clark. *No Place for Abuse: Biblical and Practical Resources to Counteract Domestic Violence.* IVP Books, 2010.

McLemore, Clinton W. *Toxic Relationships and How to Change Them.* Jossey-Bass, 2003.

Meloy, J. Reid, ed. *The Psychology of Stalking: Clinical and Forensic Perspectives.* Academic Press of San Diego, 1998.

Pike, Anne. *Danger Has a Face.* Outskirts Press, 2011.

Plantinga, Cornelius. *Not the Way It's Supposed to Be: A Breviary of Sin.* Wm. B. Eerdmans Publishing Company, 2010.

Roberts, Barbara. *Not Under Bondage: Biblical Divorce for Abuse, Adultery, and Desertion.* Maschil Press, 2008.

Simon, George K., Ph.D. *Character Disturbance: the Phenomenon of Our Age.* Parkhurst Brothers, 2011.

Stout, Martha. *The Sociopath Next Door.* Three Rivers Press, 2005.

Sutton, Ray. *Second Chance: Biblical Principles of Divorce and Remarriage.* Dominion Press, 1988.

Tracy, Steven R. *Mending the Soul: Understanding and Healing Abuse.* Zondervan, 2008.

Van Dam, Carla. *The Socially Skilled Child Molester: Differentiating the Guilty from the Falsely Accused.* Routledge, 2006.

van der Kolk, Bessel, MD. *The Body Keeps the Score: Brain, Mind, and Body in the Healing of Trauma.* Viking, 2014.

---. *Traumatic Stress: The Effects of Overwhelming Experience on Mind, Body, and Society.* The Guilford Press, 2006.

Vernick, Leslie. *The Emotionally Destructive Marriage: How to Find Your Voice and Reclaim Your Hope.* The Crown Publishing Group, 2013.

Made in the USA
Middletown, DE
10 September 2019